Off The Internet
for Everyone

An eclectic mix of stories,
jokes and inspirational pieces
Off The Internet to you!

Compiled by Tammy Wright

Off The Internet for Everyone © 2002 by Wright Opportunities, Inc.
P.O. Box 15022, Richmond, VA 23227

Proofed by: Elaine Noonan

Cover & Book Design by: Tammy Wright, The Wright Agency

Cover Models: David Wright, Brian Hunt, Bill Hudgins,
Florence Watt, Sabrena Glass, Daniel Wright,
and Wanda Durrant

All Rights Reserved

No concept or part of this publication may be reproduced, stored in a retrieval system, or transmitted in any form by any means, electronic, mechanical, photocopying, recording or otherwise, without the written permission of the publisher.

A serious effort has been made to locate sources and obtain permission to quote when required. Instances of unintentional errors or omissions, or inability to find copyright holders are sincerely regretted. Corrections will be gladly incorporated in future printings. The publishers of this publication do not claim that the statements and/or stories contained within this publication are true. They are merely items that are being emailed across the Internet.

We are an equal opportunity offender. This book or the contents within are not meant as a means to hurt, slander, or show prejudice. Its sole purpose is for entertainment only. We follow the belief that when you can laugh at yourself you can laugh with the world.

Printed in the United States of America

ISBN 0-9721167-0-2

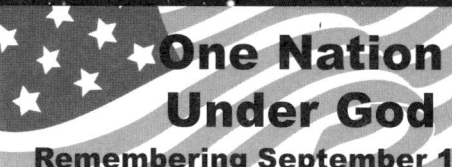

Most importantly, I thank God for his many blessings.

Also, many heartfelt and special thanks to my family and friends who have supported me through the years in all my various endeavors.

All of you have been my "Angels on Earth" in one way or another, at one time or another. Without each and everyone one of you being my driving force at various times, this would not have been possible.

I'd also especially like to thank all of you who have sent me the numerous emails with all the wonderful jokes and stories during the last couple of years that have made this book possible!

*The Lord Gave You Two Ends
One For Sitting And
One For Thinking*

*Your Success Depends
On Which You Use...
Heads You Win And
Tails You Lose!*

~Unknown

Contents

Contained within each section are selections from future books of the same name. I hope you get as much pleasure out of each section as I did!

For Blondes .... 9 - 14

For Friends .... 15 - 23

For Inspiration .... 24 - 36

For Men .... 37 - 46

For Everyone* .... 47 - 56

For Over The Hill .... 57 - 66

For Parents .... 67 - 76

For Professionals .... 77 - 86

For Rednecks .... 87 - 96

For Relationships .... 97 - 106

For Spiritual .... 107 - 115

For Women .... 117 - 126

* These are jokes and stories not intended for any specific audience.

For Blondes

The Bath

A blonde heard that milk baths make you beautiful. So she left a note for her milkman to leave 15 gallons of milk.

When the milkman read the note, he felt there must be a mistake. He thought she probably meant 1.5 gallons, so he knocked on the door to clarify the point. The blonde came to the door and the milkman said, "I found your note to leave 15 gallons of milk. Did you mean 15 gallons or 1.5 gallons?"

The blonde said, "I want 15 gallons. I'm going to fill my bathtub with milk and take a milk bath." The milkman asked, "Pasteurized?"

The blonde said, "No, just up to my chest."

The Blonde Flight Attendant

An airline captain was breaking in a very pretty new blonde flight attendant. The route they were flying had a stay-over in another city, so upon their arrival, the captain showed the attendant the best place for airline personnel to eat, shop and stay overnight. The next morning as the pilot was preparing the crew for the day's route, he noticed the new attendant was missing. He knew which room she was in at the hotel and called her up wondering what happened to her. She answered the phone sobbing, and said she couldn't get out of her room.

"You can't get out of your room?" the captain asked "Why not?" The attendant replied, "There are only three doors in here," she cried "One is the bathroom, one is the closet, and one has a sign on it that says, 'Do Not Disturb'!"

For Blondes

The Blonde Story To Beat All Blonde Stories!!!

A true story -- if she had killed herself, God forbid, she'd be a shoe-in for the Darwin Award.

Last summer, down on Lake Isabella, located in the high desert, an hour east of Bakersfield, California, a blonde, new to boating, was having a problem. No matter how hard she tried, she just couldn't get her brand new 22-ft. Bayliner to perform. It wouldn't get on a plane at all, and it was very sluggish in almost every maneuver, no matter how much power she applied. After about an hour of trying to make it go, she putted over to a nearby marina. Maybe they could tell her what was wrong. A thorough topside check revealed everything was in perfect working order. The engine ran fine, the outdrive went up and down, the prop was the correct size and pitch. So, one of the marina guys jumped into the water to check underneath. He came up choking on water, he was laughing so hard. (wait for it… REMEMBER, this is TRUE….) Under the boat, still strapped securely in place, was the trailer.

An Educated Blonde

Q. There are three girls, all in 3rd grade: one a brunette, one a redhead, and one a blonde. Which one of them has the best body?
A. The blonde, because she's 19 years old.

Q. How do you measure a blonde's I.Q.?
A. With a tire gauge.

Q. What does a blonde say after she graduates from college?
A. "Hi, welcome to McDonalds."

For Blondes

The Blonde

A blonde's car breaks down on the interstate one day so she eases over to the side of the road. She carefully steps out of the car and opens her trunk. Out jump two men in trench coats who walk to the rear of the vehicle where they begin opening their coats and exposing themselves to approaching drivers. Not surprisingly, one of the worst pile-ups in the history of this highway occurs.

It's not very long before a police car shows up. The cop, clearly enraged, runs toward the blonde of the disabled vehicle yelling, "What the hell is going on here?" " My car broke down," says the lady calmly. "What are these perverts doing here by the road?" asks the cop. And she said....... (Ready, this is good! Remember she's a blonde) "Those are my emergency flashers!" she replies.

The Misunderstanding

A highway patrolman pulled alongside a speeding car on the freeway. Glancing at the car, he was astounded to see that the blonde behind the wheel was knitting! Realizing that she was oblivious to his flashing lights and siren, the trooper cranked down his window, turned on his bullhorn and yelled, "PULLOVER!".

"NO," the blonde yelled back, "IT'S A SCARF!"

For Blondes

She Was So Blonde...

She sent me a fax with a stamp on it.

She thought a quarterback was a refund.

She tripped over the cordless phone.

She put lipstick on her forehead because she wanted to makeup her mind.

She told someone to meet her at the corner of WALK and DON'T WALK.

At the bottom of a job application where it says "sign here", she put Sagittarius.

If she spoke her mind, she'd be speechless.

When she heard that 90% of all accidents were around the home, she moved.

Did you hear about the blonde that got an AM radio? It took her months to figure out she could use it at night.

What did the blonde say when she saw the sign in front of the YMCA? "Look! They spelled MACY'S wrong!"

Why can't blondes be pharmacists? Because they can't fit the bottle in the typewriter.

What's the definition of eternity? 4 blondes at a 4-way stop.

What do you call a basement full of blondes? A whine cellar.

Why do blondes have TGIF on their shirts? "This goes in front"

And the best one for last . . .

What did the blonde say when she looked into a box of Cheerios? "OH, LOOK, donut seeds."

The Interview

The executive was interviewing a young blonde for a position in his company. He wanted to find out something about her personality so he asked, "If you could have a conversation with someone, living or dead, who would it be?"

The blonde quickly responded, "The living one."

"Space Travel"

A Russian, an American, and a blonde were talking one day.

The Russian said, "We were the first in space!"

The American said, "We were the first on the moon!"

The Blonde said, "So what, we're going to be the first on the sun!"

The Russian and the American looked at each other and shook their heads. "You can't land on the sun, you idiot! You'll burn up!" said the Russian.

To which the blonde replied, "We're not stupid, you know. We're going at night!"

For Blondes

The License

A police officer stops a blond for speeding and asks her very nicely if he could see her license. She replies in a huff, "I wish you guys would get your act together. Just yesterday you take away my license, and then today you expect me to show it to you!"

The Blonde & The Board Game

A blonde was playing Trivial Pursuit one night. It was her turn. She rolled the dice and she landed on "Science & Nature." Her question was, "If you are in a vacuum and someone calls your name, can you hear it?" She thought for a time and then asked, "Is it on or off?"

The Final Exam

The blonde reports for her university final examination which consists of "yes/no" type questions. She takes her seat in the examination hall, stares at the question paper for five minutes, and then in a fit of inspiration takes her purse out, removes a coin and starts tossing the coin and marking the answer sheet-Yes for Heads and No for Tails. Within half an hour she is all done, whereas the rest of the class is sweating it out. During the last few minutes, she is seen desperately throwing the coin in the air when the professor asks what is going on. "I finished the exam in half an hour. But I'm rechecking my answers.

For Friends

A Secret Place

Each of us has a secret place
Somewhere deep within,
A place where we go to get away,
To think things through,
To be alone,
To be ourselves.

This special place, where we keep all our deepest feelings
Becomes a storehouse of all our hopes,
All our needs, all our dreams,
All our unspoken fears,
It holds the essence of who we are
And what we want to be.

But now and then, someone comes along
And discovers a way into that place
We thought was ours alone.
And we allow that person to see,
To feel and to share
All the secrets, all the uncertainty,
And all the emotion we've stored up there.

That person adds new perspective to our hidden realm,
Then quietly settles down
In his or her own corner of our special place,
Where a part of them will live forever...

And we call that person a friend.

Dear Friend Of Mine:

I'm reading more and dusting less.

I'm sitting in the yard and admiring the view without fussing about the weeds in the garden.

I'm spending more time with my family and friends and less time working.

Whenever possible, life should be a pattern of experiences to savor, not to endure.

I'm trying to recognize these moments now and cherish them.

I'm not "saving" anything.

We use our good china and crystal for every special event such as losing a pound, getting the sink unstopped, or seeing the first Amaryllis blossom.

I wear my good blazer to the market. My theory is if I look prosperous, I can shell out $28.49 for one small bag of groceries.

I'm not saving my good perfume for special parties, but wearing it for clerks in the hardware store and tellers at the bank.

"Someday" and "one of these days" are losing their grip on my vocabulary. If it's worth seeing or hearing or doing, I want to see and hear and do it now.

I'm not sure what others would've done had they known they wouldn't be here for the tomorrow that we all take for granted.

I think they would have called family members and a few close friends. They might have called a few former friends to apologize and mend fences for past squabbles.

For Friends

It's those little things left undone that would make me angry if I knew my hours were limited. Angry because I hadn't written certain letters that I intended to write one of these days. Angry and sorry that I didn't tell my husband and parents often enough how much I truly love them.

I'm trying very hard not to put off, hold back, and save anything that would add laughter and lustre to our lives.

And every morning when I open my eyes, I tell myself that it is special. Every day, every minute, every breath truly is a gift.

People say true friends must always hold hands, but true friends don't need to hold hands because they know the other hand will always be there.

I don't believe in Miracles. I RELY on them.

Children are more often than not a better example of how we should live our lives and treat others than what we are to them!
~Tammy Wright

For Friends

My Special List

I have a list of folks I know... all written in a book, and every now and then.. I go and take a look.

That is when I realize these names... they are a part, not of the book they're written in... but taken from the heart.

For each name stands for someone... who has crossed my path sometime, and in that meeting they have become... the reason and the rhyme.

Although it sounds fantastic... for me to make this claim, I really am composed... of each remembered name.

Although you're not aware... of any special link, just knowing you, has shaped my life... more than you could think.

So please don't think my greeting... as just a mere routine, your name was not... forgotten in between.

For when I send a greeting via email... that is addressed to you, it is because you're on the list... of folks I'm indebted to.

So whether I have known you... for many days or few, in some ways you have a part... in shaping things I do.

I am but a total... of many folks I've met, you are a friend I would prefer... never to forget.

Thank you for being my friend!

For Friends

Around The Corner I Have A Friend

Around the corner I have a friend
In this great city that has no end,
Yet the days go by and weeks rush on,
And before I know it, a year is gone

And I never see my old friend's face,
For life is a swift and terrible race,
She knows I like her just as well,
As in the days when I rang her bell,
And she rang mine..

We were much younger then
And now we are busy, tired women..
Tired of playing a foolish game,
Tired of trying to make a name

"Tomorrow" I say "I will call on Jim"
"Just to show that I'm thinking of him."
But tomorrow comes and tomorrow goes
And distance between us grows and grows..

Around the corner- yet miles away,
Here's a telegram sir, "Jim died today."

And that's what we get and deserve in the end..
Around the corner, a vanished friend..

Continued on next page

For Friends

Continued from previous page

If you love someone, tell him...
Remember always to say what you mean..
Never be afraid to express yourself..
Take this opportunity to tell someone
what he means to you..

Seize the day and have no regrets..
Most importantly, stay close to your
friends and family, for they have helped
make you the person that you are today
and are what it's all about anyway

Pass this along to your friends.
The difference between expressing love and
having regrets is that the regrets may stay
around forever..

Written With A Pen

Sealed with a kiss. If you are my friend, please answer this:
Are we friends or are we not? You told me once but I forgot.
So tell me now and tell me true so I can say.... "I'm here for you."
Of all the friends I've ever met, you're the one I won't forget.
And if I die before you do, I'll go to heaven and wait for you.
I'll give the angels back their wings and risk the loss of everything just
to prove my friendship is true.. to have a friend like you!

For Friends

The ABCs Of Friendship...

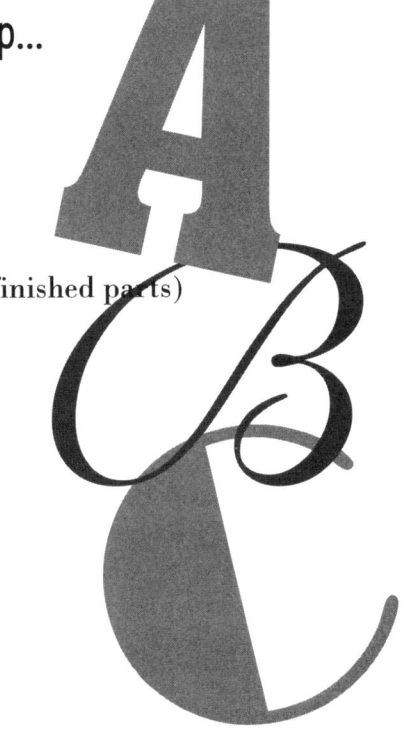

(A)ccepts you as you are
(B)elieves in "you"
(C)alls you just to say "HI"
(D)oesn't give up on you
(E)nvisions the whole of you (even the unfinished parts)
(F)orgives your mistakes
(G)ives unconditionally
(H)elps you
(I)nvites you over
(J)ust wants to "be" with you
(K)eeps you close at heart
(L)oves you for who you are
(M)akes a difference in your life
(N)ever judges
(O)ffers support
(P)icks you up
(Q)uiets your fears
(R)aises your spirits
(S)ays nice things about you
(T)ells you the truth when you need to hear it
(U)nderstands you
(V)alues you
(W)alks beside you
(X)-plains things you don't understand
(Y)ells when you won't listen and
(Z)aps you back to reality

For Friends

Time & Friends

Imagine there is a bank that credits your account each morning with $86,400.

It carries over no balance from day to day.

Every evening deletes whatever part of the balance you failed to use during the day.

What would you do? Draw out ALL OF IT, of course!!!!

Well, each of us has such a bank. Its name is TIME.

Every morning, it credits you with 86,400 seconds.

Every night it writes off, as lost, whatever of this you have failed to invest to good purpose.

It carries over no balance. It allows no overdraft.

Each day it opens a new account for you.

Each night it burns the remains of the day.

If you fail to use the day's deposits, the loss is yours.

There is no going back.

There is no drawing against tomorrow.

You must live in the present, on today's deposits.

Invest it so as to get from it the utmost in health, happiness, and success!

The clock is running. Make the most of today.

To realize the value of ONE YEAR, ask a student who failed a grade.

To realize the value of ONE MONTH, ask a mother who gave birth to a premature baby.

For Friends

To realize the value of ONE WEEK, ask the editor of a weekly newspaper.

To realize the value of ONE HOUR, ask the lovers who are waiting to meet.

To realize the value of ONE MINUTE, ask a person who missed the train.

To realize the value of ONE SECOND, ask a person who just avoided an accident.

To realize the value of ONE MILLISECOND, ask the person who won a silver medal in the Olympics.

Treasure every moment that you have! And treasure it more because you shared it with someone special, special enough to spend your time with.

And remember that time waits for no one.

Friends are a very rare jewel, indeed. They make you smile and encourage you to succeed.

They lend an ear, they share a word of praise, and they always want to open their hearts to you.

For Inspiration

What I've Learned - 101

I've learned that you can tell a lot about a person by the way he/she handles 3 things:- a rainy day, lost luggage, and tangled Christmas lights.

I've learned that, regardless of your relationship with your parents, you will miss them when they are gone from your life.

I've learned that making a "living" is not the same as making a life.

I've learned that life sometimes gives you a second chance.

I've learned that you shouldn't go through life with a catchers mitt on both hands. You need to be able to throw something back.

I've learned that if you pursue happiness, it will elude you. But, if you focus on your family, your friends, and the needs of others, your work and doing the very best you can, happiness will find you.

I've learned that whenever I decide something with an open heart, I usually make the right decision.

I've learned that every day, you should reach out and touch someone. People love that human touch-holding hands, a warm hug, or just a friendly pat on the back.

I've learned that I still have a lot to learn.

I've learned that people will forget what you said, people will forget what you did, but people never will forget how you made them feel.

On a positive note, I have learned that, no matter what happens, how bad it seems today, life goes on, and it will be better tomorrow.

For Inspiration

Wings Of A Butterfly

A man found a cocoon of a butterfly. One day a small opening appeared. He sat and watched the butterfly for several hours as it struggled to force its body through that little hole. Then it seemed to stop making any progress. It appeared as if it had gotten as far it could, and it could go no further. So the man decided to help the butterfly. He took a pair of scissors and snipped off the remaining bit of the cocoon. The butterfly then emerged easily. But it had a swollen body and small shriveled wings. The man continued to watch the butterfly because expected that, at any moment, the wings would enlarge and expand to be able to support the body, which would contract in time. Neither happened! In fact, the butterfly spent the rest of its life crawling around with a swollen body and shriveled wings. It never was able to fly.

What the man, in his kindness and haste, did not understand was that the restricting cocoon and the struggle required for the butterfly to get through the tiny opening were God's way of forcing fluid from the body of the butterfly into its wings so that it would be ready for flight once it achieved its freedom from the cocoon.

Sometimes struggles are exactly what we need in our lives. If God allowed us to go through our lives without any obstacles, it would cripple us. We would not be as strong as what we could have been. We could never fly!

For Inspiration

Carrot, Egg Or Coffee Bean?

A young woman went to her mother and told her about her life and how things were so hard for her. She did not know how she was going to make it and wanted to give up. She was tired of fighting and struggling. It seemed that as one problem was solved a new one arose. Her mother took her to the kitchen.

She filled three pots with water and placed each on a high fire. Soon the pots came to a boil. In the first, she placed carrots, in the second she placed eggs and the last she placed ground coffee beans. She let them sit and boil, without saying a word. In about twenty minutes she turned off the burners. She fished the carrots out and placed them in a bowl. She pulled the eggs out and placed them in a bowl. Then she ladled the coffee out and placed it in a bowl. Turning to her daughter, she asked, "Tell me, what do you see?"

"Carrots, eggs, and coffee," she replied. She brought her closer and asked her to feel the carrots. She did and noted that they were soft. She then asked her to take an egg and break it. After pulling off the shell, she observed the hard-boiled egg. Finally, she asked her to sip the coffee. The daughter smiled as she tasted its rich aroma. The daughter then asked, "What does it mean, mother?"

Her mother explained that each of these objects had faced the same adversity—boiling water—but each reacted differently. The carrot went in strong, hard and unrelenting. However after being subjected to the boiling water, it softened and became weak. The egg had been fragile. Its thin outer shell had protected its liquid interior. But, after sitting through the boiling water, its inside became hardened!

For Inspiration

The ground coffee beans were unique, however. After they were in the boiling water they had changed the water.

"Which are you?" she asked her daughter. " When adversity knocks on your door, how do you respond? Are you a carrot, an egg, or a coffee bean?"

Think of this: Which am I? Am I the carrot that seems strong, but with pain and adversity, do I wilt and become soft and lose my strength? Am I the egg that starts with a malleable heart, but changes with the heat? Did I have a fluid spirit, but after death, a breakup, a financial hardship or does my shell look the same, but on the inside am I bitter and tough with a stiff spirit and a hardened heart?

Or am I like the coffee bean? The bean actually changes the hot water, the very circumstance that brings the pain. When the water gets hot, it releases the fragrance and flavor. If you are like the bean, when things are at their worst, you get better and change the situation around you. When the hours are the darkest and trials are their greatest, do you elevate to another level? How do you handle adversity?

ARE YOU A CARROT, AN EGG, OR A COFFEE BEAN?

Yesterday is history.. Tomorrow a mystery.. Today is a gift.. That's why it's called the present! Live and savor every moment… this is not a dress rehearsal!

For Inspiration

Change Begins With Choice

Any day we wish, we can discipline ourselves to change it all. Any day we wish, we can open the book that will open our mind to new knowledge. Any day we wish, we can start a new activity. Any day we wish, we can start the process of life change. We can do it immediately, or next week, or next month, or next year.

We can also do nothing. We can pretend rather than perform. And if the idea of having to change ourselves makes us uncomfortable, we can remain as we are. We can choose rest over labor, entertainment over education, delusion over truth, and doubt over confidence. The choices are ours to make. But while we curse the effect, we continue to nourish the cause. As Shakespeare uniquely observed, "The fault is not in the stars, but in ourselves." We created our circumstances by our past choices. We have both the ability and the responsibility to make better choices beginning today. Those who are in search of the good life do not need more answers or more time to think things over to reach better conclusions. They need the truth. They need the whole truth. And they need nothing but the truth.

We cannot allow our errors in judgment, repeated every day, to lead us down the wrong path. We must keep coming back to those basics that make the biggest difference in how our life works out. And then we must make the very choices that will bring life, happiness and joy into our daily lives.

And if I may be so bold as to offer my last piece of advice for someone seeking and needing to make changes in his life - If you don't like how things are, change them ! You're not a tree. You have the ability to totally transform every area in your life - and it all begins with your very own _power of choice!!_

For Inspiration

If I Had My Life To Live Over

by Erma Bombeck (Written after she found out she was dying from cancer.)

I would have gone to bed when I was sick instead of pretending the earth would go into a holding pattern if I weren't there for the day.

I would have burned the pink candle sculpted like a rose before it melted in storage. I would have talked less and listened more.

I would have invited friends over to dinner even if the carpet was stained, or the sofa faded.

I would have eaten the popcorn in the 'good' living room and worried much less about the dirt when someone wanted to light a fire in the fireplace.

I would have taken the time to listen to my grandfather ramble about his youth.

I would have shared more of the responsibility carried by my husband.

I would never have insisted the car windows be rolled up on a summer day because my hair had just been teased and sprayed.

I would have sat on the lawn with my children and not worried about grass stains.

I would have cried and laughed less while watching television and more while watching life.

I would never have bought anything just because it was practical, wouldn't show soil, or was guaranteed to last a lifetime.

Continued on next page

For Inspiration

Continued from previous page

Instead of wishing away nine months of pregnancy, I'd have cherished every moment and realized that the wonderment growing inside me was the only chance in life to assist God in a miracle.

When my kids kissed me impetuously, I would never have said, "Later. Now go get washed up for dinner."

There would have been more "I love you's." More "I'm sorry's."

But mostly, given another shot at life, I would seize every minute... look at it and really see it ... live it ... and never give it back.

Stop sweating the small stuff.

Don't worry about who doesn't like you, who has more, or who's doing what. Instead, let's cherish the relationships we have with those who do love us.

Let's think about what God HAS blessed us with. And what we are doing each day to promote ourselves mentally, physically, emotionally, as well as spiritually. Life is too short to let it pass you by. We only have one shot at this and then it's gone.

by Erma Bombeck

For Inspiration

Feelings

Once upon a time there was an island where all the feelings lived: happiness, sadness, knowledge, and all the others, including love.

One day it was announced to all of the feelings that the island was going to sink to the bottom of the ocean. So all the feelings prepared their boats to leave.

Love was the only one that stayed. She wanted to preserve the island paradise until the last possible moment. When the island was almost totally under, Love decided it was time to leave. She began looking for someone to ask for help.

Just then Richness was passing by in a grand boat. Love asked, "Richness, can I come with you on your boat?"

Richness answered, " I'm sorry, but there is a lot of silver and gold on my boats and there would be no room for you anywhere."

Then Love decided to ask Vanity for help who was passing in a beautiful vessel. Love cried out, "Vanity, help me please."

"I can't help you." Vanity said, "You are all wet and will damage my beautiful boat."

Next, Love saw Sadness passing by. Love said, "Sadness, please let me go with you." Sadness answered, "Love, I'm sorry, but I just need to be alone now."

Then, Love saw Happiness. Love cried out, "Happiness, please take me with you." But Happiness was so overjoyed that he didn't hear Love calling to him.

Continued on next page

For Inspiration

Continued from previous page

Love began to cry. Then she heard a voice say, "Come, Love I will take you with me." It was an elder.

Love felt so blessed and overjoyed that she forgot to ask the elder his name.

When they arrived on land, the elder went on his way.

Love realized how much she owed the elder.

Love then found Knowledge and asked, "Who was it that helped me?" "It was Time," Knowledge answered.

"But why did Time help me when no one else would?" Love asked.

Knowledge smiled and with deep wisdom and sincerity answered, "Because only Time is capable of understanding how great Love is."

~Author unknown

Send submissions & feedback to: mailto:womenswords@memail.com

For Inspiration

First Most Important Lesson

During my second month of nursing school, our professor gave us a pop quiz. I was a conscientious student and had breezed through the questions, until I read the last one: "What is the first name of the woman who cleans the school?"

Surely, this was some kind of joke. I had seen the cleaning woman several times. She was tall, dark-haired and in her 50s, but how would I know her name? I handed in my paper, leaving the last question blank. Just before class ended, one student asked if the last question would count toward our quiz grade. "Absolutely," said the professor. "In your careers, you will meet many people.. all are significant. They deserve your attention and care, even if all you do is smile and say 'hello'."

"I've never forgotten that lesson. I also learned her name was Dorothy.

Second Important Lesson: Pickup In The Rain

One night, at 11:30 PM, an older African American woman was standing on the side of an Alabama highway trying to endure a lashing rainstorm. Her car had broken down, and she desperately needed a ride.

Soaking wet, she decided to flag down the next car. A young white man stopped to help her, generally unheard of in those conflict-filled 1960s. The man took her to safety, helped her get assistance, and put her into

Continued on next page

33

For Inspiration

Continued from previous page

a taxicab. She seemed to be in a big hurry, but wrote down his address and thanked him. Seven days went by and a knock came on the man's door. To his surprise, a giant console color TV was delivered to his home. A special note was attached. It read: "Thank you so much for assisting me on the highway the other night. The rain drenched not only my clothes, but also my spirits. Then you came along. Because of you, I was able to make it to my dying husband's bedside just before he passed away.

God bless you for helping me and unselfishly serving others."

Sincerely,

Mrs. Nat King Cole.

Third Important Lesson: Always Remember Those Who Serve You

In the days when an ice cream sundae cost much less, a 10-year-old boy entered a hotel coffee shop and sat at a table. A waitress put a glass of water in front of him. "How much is an ice cream sundae?" he asked. "Fifty cents," replied the waitress. The little boy pulled his hand out of his pocket and studied the coins in it.

"Well, how much is a plain dish of ice cream?" he inquired. By now, more people were waiting for a table and the waitress was growing impatient.

"Thirty-five cents," she brusquely replied. The little boy again

For Inspiration

counted his coins. "I'll have the plain ice cream," he said. The waitress brought the ice cream, put the bill on the table and walked away. The boy finished the ice cream, paid the cashier and left. When the waitress came back, she began to cry as she wiped down the table. There, placed neatly beside the empty dish, were two nickels and five pennies. You see, he couldn't have the sundae because he had to have enough left to leave her a tip.

Fourth Important Lesson: The Obstacle In Our Path

In ancient times, a king had a boulder placed on a roadway. Then he hid himself and watched to see if anyone would remove the huge rock. Some of the king's wealthiest merchants and courtiers came by and simply walked around it. Many loudly blamed the king for not keeping the roads clear, but none did anything about getting the stone out of the way. Then a peasant came along carrying a load of vegetables.

Upon approaching the boulder, the peasant laid down his burden and tried to move the stone to the side of the road. After much pushing and straining, he finally succeeded. After the peasant picked up his load of vegetables, he noticed a purse lying in the road where the boulder had been. The purse contained many gold coins and a note from the king indicating that the gold was for the person who removed the boulder from the roadway. The peasant learned what many of us never understand.

Every obstacle presents an opportunity to improve our condition.

Continued on next page

For Inspiration

Continued from previous page

Fifth Important Lesson: Giving When It Counts

Many years ago, when I worked as a volunteer at a hospital, I got to know a little girl named Liz who was suffering from a rare and serious disease. Her only chance of recovery appeared to be a blood transfusion from her 5 year-old brother, who had miraculously survived the same disease and had developed the antibodies needed to combat the illness. The doctor explained the situation to her little brother, and asked the little boy if he would be willing to give his blood to his sister. I saw him hesitate for only a moment before taking a deep breath and saying, "Yes, I'll do it if it will save her…!"

As the transfusion progressed, he lay in bed next to his sister and smiled, as we all did, seeing the color returning to her cheeks. Then his face grew pale and his smile faded. He looked up at the doctor and asked with a trembling voice, "Will I start to die right away?"

Being young, the little boy had misunderstood the doctor; he thought he was going to have to give his sister all of his blood in order to save her. You see, understanding and attitude, after all, is everything.

For Men

What Would You Like To Hear...

Tragically, three friends die in a car crash, and they find themselves at the gates of heaven. Before entering, they are each asked a question by St. Peter.

"When you are in your casket and friends and family are mourning you, what would you like to hear them say about you?" asks St. Peter.

The first guy says, "I would like to hear them say that I was a great doctor of my time, and a great family man." The second guy says, "I would like to hear that I was a wonderful husband and school teacher who made a huge difference in our children of tomorrow."

The last guy replies, "I would like to hear them say...... LOOK!!! HE'S MOVING!!!!!"

How many men does it take to open a beer?
None. It should be open when she brings it.

Why do women have smaller feet than men?
So they can stand closer to the kitchen sink.

Why do men pass gas more than women?
Because women won't shut up long enough to build up pressure.

For Men

The Difference Between Men & Women

MEN & WOMEN COMPARED NICKNAMES - If Laura, Suzanne, Debra and Rose go out for lunch, they will call each other Laura, Suzanne, Debra and Rose. If Mike, Charlie, Bob and John go out, they will affectionately refer to each other as Fat Boy, Godzilla, Peanut-Head and Scrappy.

EATING OUT - When the bill arrives, Mike, Charlie, Bob and John will each throw in $20, though it's only for $32.50. None of them will have anything smaller, and none will actually admit they want change back. When the girls get their bill, out come the pocket calculators.

MONEY - A man will pay $2 for a $1 item he wants. A woman will pay $1 for a $2 item that she doesn't want.

BATHROOMS - A man has six items in his bathroom: a toothbrush, shaving cream, razor, a bar of soap, and a towel from the Holiday Inn. The average number of items in the typical woman's bathroom is 337. A man would not be able to identify most of these items.

ARGUMENTS - A woman has the last word in any argument. Anything a man says after that is the beginning of a new argument.

CATS - Women love cats. Men say they love cats, but when women aren't looking, men kick cats.

FUTURE - A woman worries about the future until she gets a husband. A man never worries about the future until he gets a wife.

SUCCESS - A successful man is one who makes more money than his wife can spend. A successful woman is one who can find such a man.

For Men

MARRIAGE - A woman marries a man expecting he will change, but he doesn't. A man marries a woman expecting that she won't change and she does.

DRESSING UP - A woman will dress up to go shopping, water the plants, empty the garbage, answer the phone, read a book, and get the mail. A man will dress up for weddings and funerals.

NATURAL - Men wake up as good-looking as they went to bed. Women somehow deteriorate during the night.

OFFSPRING- Ah, children. A woman knows all about her children. She knows about dentist appointments and romances, best friends, favorite foods, secret fears and hopes and dreams. A man is vaguely aware of some short people living in the house.

THOUGHT FOR THE DAY - Any married man should forget his mistakes. There's no use in two people remembering the same thing.

If your dog is barking at the back door and your wife is yelling at the front door, who do you let in first?
The dog of course. At least he'll shut up after you let him in.

I married Miss Right.
I just didn't know her first name was Always.

For Men

You Can Tell It Is Going To Be A Rotten Day When...

You wake up face down on the pavement.

You call Suicide Prevention and they put you on hold.

You see a "60 Minutes" news team waiting in your office.

Your birthday cake collapses from the weight of the candles.

You want to put on the clothes you wore home from the party and there aren't any.

You turn on the news and they're showing emergency routes out of the city.

Your twin brother forgot your birthday.

Your car horn goes off accidentally and remains stuck as you follow a group of Hell's Angels on the freeway.

The bird singing outside your window is a buzzard.

You call your answering service and they tell you it's none of your business.

Your blind date turns out to be your ex-wife.

Your income tax check bounces.

You put both contact lenses in the same eye.

Your pet rock snaps at you.

Your wife says, good morning, Bill" and your name is George.

For Men

The Best Reasons Not To Exercise

1) My grandmother started walking five miles a day when she was 60. She's 97 now & we don't know where the hell she is.

2) The only reason I might take up jogging is so that I could hear heavy breathing again.

3) I joined a health club last year, spent about 400 bucks. Haven't lost a pound, apparently you have to show up.

4) I'd have to exercise in the morning before my brain figured out what I was doing.

5) I don't exercise at all. If God meant us to touch our toes, he would have put them further up on our body.

6) I like long walks, especially when they are taken by people who annoy me.

7) I have flabby thighs, but fortunately my stomach covers them.

8) The advantage of exercising every day is that you might die a little healthier.

9) If you are going to try cross-country skiing, start with a small country.

10) I don't jog. It causes the ice to jump right out of my glass.

—— 🐌 ——

I haven't spoken to my wife for 18 months;
I don't like to interrupt her.

Our last fight was my fault: My wife asked me "What's on the TV?"
I said, "Dust!"

For Men

Ten Things To Learn From A Dog

1. When loved ones come home, always run to greet them.
2. Allow the experience of fresh air and the wind in your face to be pure ecstasy.
3. Let others know when they've invaded your privacy.
4. Take naps and stretch before rising.
5. Run, romp, and play daily.
6. On hot days, drink lots of water and lay under a shady tree.
7. When you're happy, dance around and wag your entire body.
8. No matter how often you're scolded, don't buy into the guilt thing and pout... run right back out and make friends.
9. Delight in the simple joy of a long walk.
10. Eat with gusto and enthusiasm. Stop when you have had enough.
11. Be loyal.
12. Never pretend to be something you're not.
13. If what you want lies buried, dig until you find it.

For Men

I Have A Riddle For You

Schwartzenegger has a big one,

Michael J. Fox has a small one,

Madonna doesn't have one,

The Pope has one but doesn't use it,

Clinton uses his all the time,

Mickey Mouse has an unusual one,

George Burns' was hot,

Liberace never used his on women,

Jerry Seinfeld is very, very proud of his,

We never saw Lucy use Desi's

What is it?

Answer below...

Get your mind out of the gutter.

The answer is: " A Last Name"

For Men

Not As They Appear

An extraordinarily handsome man decided he had the God-given responsibility to marry the perfect woman so they could produce children beyond comparison. With that as his mission he began searching for the perfect woman. After a diligent, but fruitless, search up and down the East Coast, he started to head West. Shortly thereafter he met a farmer who had three stunning, gorgeous daughters that positively took his breath away. So he explained his mission to the farmer, asking for permission to marry one of them. The farmer simply replied, "They're all looking to get married, so you came to the right place. Look them over and select the one you want." The man dated the first daughter. The next day the farmer asked for the man's opinion.

Well," said the man, "she's just a weeeeee bit, not that you can hardly notice... but pigeon-toed." The farmer nodded and suggested the man date one of the other girls. So the man went out with the second daughter. The next day, the farmer again asked how things went. "Well," the man replied, "she's just a weeeee bit, not that you can hardly tell... cross-eyed."

The farmer nodded and suggested he date the third girl to see if things might be better. So he did. The next morning the man rushed in exclaiming, "She's perfect, just perfect! She's the one I want to marry!" So they were wed right away. Months later the baby was born. When the man visited the nursery he was horrified. The baby was the ugliest, most pathetic human you can imagine. He rushed to his father-in-law asking how such a thing could happen considering the parents.

"Well," explained the farmer, "she was just a weeeee bit, not that you could hardly tell... pregnant when you met her."

For Men

Tid Bits And What's Up With That Stuff

If Fed Ex and UPS were to merge, would they call it Fed UP?

I believe five out of four people have trouble with fractions.

If quitters never win, and winners never quit, what fool came up with, "Quit while you're ahead?"

Do Lipton Tea employees take coffee breaks?

What hair color do they put on the driver's licenses of bald men?

I was thinking that women should put pictures of missing husbands on beer cans.

I was thinking about how people seem to read the Bible a whole lot more as they get older, and then it dawned on me . . . they were cramming for their finals.

I thought about how mothers feed their babies with little tiny spoons and forks so I wonder what Chinese mothers use. Perhaps toothpicks?

Why do they put pictures of criminals up in the post office? What are we supposed to do . . . write to these men? Why don't they just put their pictures on the postage stamps so the mailmen could look for them while they delivered the mail?

Never agree to plastic surgery if the doctor's office is full of portraits by Picasso.

How much deeper would oceans be if sponges didn't live there?

If it's true that we are here to help others, then what exactly are the OTHERS here for?

Continued on next page

For Men

Continued from previous page

You never really learn to swear until you learn to drive.

Clones are people two.

If a man says something in the woods and there are no women there, is he still wrong?

No one ever says "It's only a game." when their team is winning.

If you can't be kind, at least have the decency to be vague.

Ever wonder what the speed of lightning would be if it didn't zigzag?

Last night I played a blank tape at full blast. The mime next door went nuts.

If a person with multiple personalities threatens suicide, is that considered a hostage situation?

If a cow laughed, would milk come out her nose?

If olive oil comes from olives, where does baby oil come from?

For Everyone

Helpful Household Hints...

Stuff a miniature marshmallow in the bottom of a sugar cone to prevent ice-cream drips.

Use a meat baster to "squeeze" your pancake batter onto the hot griddle into perfect shaped pancakes every time.

To keep potatoes from budding, place an apple in the bag with the potatoes.

To prevent eggshells from cracking, add a pinch of salt to the water before hard-boiling.

Run your hands under cold water before pressing Rice Krispies treats in the pan-the marshmallow won't stick to your fingers.

To get the most juice out of fresh lemons, bring them to room temperature and roll them under your palm against the kitchen counter before squeezing.

To easily remove burnt-on food from your skillet, simply add a drop or two of dish soap and enough water to cover bottom of pan, and bring to a boil on stove top-the skillet will be much easier to clean.

Spray your Tupperware with nonstick cooking spray before pouring in tomato-based sauces-no more stains.

When a cake recipe calls for flouring the baking pan, use a bit of the dry cake mix instead-no white mess on the outside of the cake.

Continued on next page

For Everyone

Continued from previous page

If you over-salt a dish while it's still cooking, drop in a peeled potato it absorbs the excess salt for an instant "fix me up."

Wrap celery in aluminum foil when putting in the refrigerator-it will keep for weeks.

Brush beaten egg white over pie crust before baking to yield a beautiful, glossy finish.

When boiling corn on the cob, add a pinch of sugar to help bring out the corn's natural sweetness.

To determine whether an egg is fresh, immerse it in a pan of cool, salted water. If it sinks, it is fresh; if it rises to the surface, throw it away.

Cure for headaches: Take a lime, cut it in half and rub it on your forehead. The throbbing will go.

Don't throw out all that leftover wine: freeze into ice cubes for future use in casseroles and sauces.

If you have problem opening jars: try using latex dishwashing gloves. They give a non-slip grip that makes opening jars easy.

Potatoes will take food stains off your fingers. Just slice and rub raw potato on the stains and rinse with water.

To get rid of itch from mosquito bite try applying soap on the area for instant relief.

For Everyone

Ants, ants, ants everywhere ... Well, they are said to never cross a chalk line. So get your chalk out and draw a line on the floor wherever ants tend to march.

Use air-freshener to clean mirrors: It does a good job and better still, leaves a lovely smell to the shine.

When you get a splinter, reach for the scotch tape before resorting to tweezers or a needle. Simply put the scotch tape over the splinter, then pull it off. Scotch tape removes most splinters painlessly and easily.

NOW Look what you can do with Alka Seltzer:

- Clean a toilet. Drop in two Alka-Seltzer tablets, wait twenty minutes, brush, and flush. The citric acid and effervescent action clean vitreous china.

- Clean a vase. To remove a stain from the bottom of a glass vase or cruet, fill with water and drop in two Alka-Seltzer tablets.

- Polish jewelry. Drop two Alka-Seltzer tablets into a glass of water and immerse the jewelry for two minutes.

- Clean a thermos bottle. Fill the bottle with water, drop in four Alka-Seltzer tablets, and let soak for an hour (or longer, if necessary).

- Unclog a drain. Clear the sink drain by dropping three Alka-Seltzer tablets down the drain followed by a cup of Heinz White Vinegar. Wait a few minutes, then run the hot water.

For Everyone

Sixth Grade Science Lesson:

"Who can tell me which organ of the human body expands to 10 times its usual size when stimulated?" Nobody raises a hand, so he calls on the first student to look his way. "Mary, can you tell me which organ of the human body expands to 10 times its usual size when stimulated?"

Mary stands up, blushing furiously. "Sir, how dare you ask such a question?" she says. "I'm going to complain to my parents, who will complain to the principal, who will have you fired!"

Mr. Sampson is shocked by Mary's reaction, but undaunted. He asks the class the question again, and this time Sam raises his hand. "Yes, Sam?" says Mr. Sampson.

"Sir, the correct answer is the iris of the human eye."

"Very good, Sam. Thank you." Mr. Sampson then turns to Mary and says, "Mary, I have 3 things to tell you: First, it's clear that you have NOT done your homework. Second, you have a DIRTY mind. And third, I fear one day you are going to be sadly disappointed."

For Everyone

New Liquor Labels

Due to increasing products liability litigation, American liquor manufacturers have accepted the FDA's suggestion that the following warning labels be placed immediately on all containers:

WARNING: The consumption of alcohol may make you think you are whispering when you are not.

WARNING: The consumption of alcohol is a major factor in dancing like a idiot.

WARNING: The consumption of alcohol may cause you to tell your friends over and over again that you love them.

WARNING: The consumption of alcohol may cause you to think you can sing.

WARNING: The consumption of alcohol may lead you to believe that ex-lovers are really dying for you to telephone them at four in the morning.

WARNING: The consumption of alcohol may make you think you can logically converse with other members of the opposite sex without spitting.

WARNING: The consumption of alcohol may make you think you have mystical Kung Fu powers, resulting in your getting your ass kicked.

WARNING: The consumption of alcohol may cause you to roll over in the morning and see something really scary.

Continued on next page

For Everyone

Continued from previous page

WARNING: The consumption of alcohol is the leading cause of inexplicable rug burns on the forehead, knees and lower back.

WARNING: The consumption of alcohol may create the illusion that you are tougher, smarter, faster and better looking than most people.

WARNING: The consumption of alcohol may lead you to believe you are invisible.

WARNING: The consumption of alcohol may lead you to think people are laughing WITH you.

WARNING: The consumption of alcohol may cause a disturbance in the time-space continuum, whereby periods of time may seem to literally disappear.

WARNING: The consumption of alcohol may cause pregnancy!

Points To Ponder:

Old accountants never die, they just lose their balance.
Crime doesn't pay, but the hours are optional.
Never put off until tomorrow what you can put off altogether.
Procrastination is the thief of time, especially if you can't spell it.
Important letters that contain no errors will develop errors in the mail.
If it weren't for the last minute, nothing would ever get done.
Help Wanted: Telepath. You know where to apply.

For Everyone

The Outhouse

The service station trade was slow so the owner sat around, with whittling with a sharpened knife as cedar shavings piled on the ground.

No modern facilities had they, the log across the hill led to a shack, marked His and Hers that sat against the hill.

"Where is the ladies restroom, sir?" the female customer inquired. The owner leaning back, said not a word but whittled on, and nodded toward the shack.

With quickened step she entered there but only stayed a minute, until she screamed, just like a snake or spider might be in it.

With startled look and beet red face she bounded through the door, and headed quickly for the car just like the three gals before.

She missed the foot log - jumped the stream the owner gave a shout, as her silk stockings, down at her knees caught on a sassafras sprout.

She tripped and fell - got up, and then in obvious disgust, ran to the car, stepped on the gas, and faded in the dust.

Of course we all desired to know what made the gals run as they did. We soon found out the whittling owner knew.

For he'd devised a speaking system and to make the thing complete, he tied a speaker on the wall beneath the toilet seat.

He'd wait until the gals got set and then the devilish tyke, would stop his whittling long enough, to speak into the mike.

And as she sat, a voice below struck terror, fright and fear, "Will you please use the other hole, *we're painting under here!*"

For Everyone

How To Bathe A Cat!

1. Thoroughly clean the toilet.

2. Add the required amount of shampoo to the toilet water, and have both lids lifted.

3. Obtain the cat and soothe him while you carry him towards the bathroom.

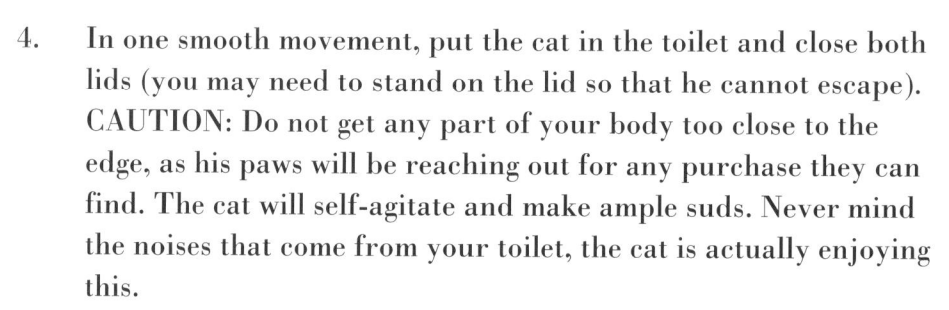

4. In one smooth movement, put the cat in the toilet and close both lids (you may need to stand on the lid so that he cannot escape). CAUTION: Do not get any part of your body too close to the edge, as his paws will be reaching out for any purchase they can find. The cat will self-agitate and make ample suds. Never mind the noises that come from your toilet, the cat is actually enjoying this.

5. Flush the toilet three or four times. This provides a "power wash" and "rinse" which I have found to be quite effective.

6. Have someone open the door to the outside and ensure that there are no people between the toilet and the outside door.

7. Stand behind the toilet as far as you can, and quickly lift both lids.

8. The now-clean cat will rocket out of the toilet, and run outside where he will dry himself.

Sincerely,

The Dog

For Everyone

Polish Air Disaster

Poland's worst air disaster occurred today when a small two-seater Cessna plane crashed into a cemetery early this afternoon in central Poland. Polish search and rescue workers have recovered 826 bodies so far and expect that number to climb as digging continues into the evening.

I Just Love Corny Jokes...

How do crazy people go through the forest?
They take the psycho path.

How do you get holy water?
You boil the hell out of it.

What do fish say when they hit a concrete wall?
Damn!

What do Eskimos get from sitting on the ice too long?
Polaroids.

What do you call cheese that isn't yours?
Nacho cheese.

Continued on next page

For Everyone

Continued from previous page

What do you get from a pampered cow?
Spoiled milk.

What do you get when you cross a snowman with a vampire?
Frostbite.

What lies at the bottom of the ocean and twitches?
A nervous wreck.

Where do you find a dog with no legs?
Right where you left him.

What's the difference between a bad golfer and a bad skydiver?
A bad golfer goes whack, dang. A bad skydiver goes dang, whack.

What do you call skydiving lawyers?
Skeet.

What goes clop, clop, clop, bang, bang, clop clop clop?
An Amish drive-by shooting.

How is a Texas tornado and a Tennessee divorce the same?
Somebody's gonna lose a trailer.

For Over The Hill

The Home Cure

A man was walking down the street when he noticed his grandfather sitting on porch, in the rocking chair, with nothing on from the waist down.

"Grandpa what are you doing?" he exclaimed. The old man looked off in the distance without answering.

"Grandpa, what are you doing sitting out here with nothing on below the waist?" he asked again. The old man slowly looked at him and said, "Well, last week I sat out here with no shirt on, and I got a stiff neck. This is your Grandma's idea."

Overboard

An elderly couple was on a cruise, and it was really stormy. They were standing on the back of the boat watching the moon, when a wave came up and washed the old man overboard. They searched for days and couldn't find him, So the captain sent the old woman back to shore with the promise that he would notify her as soon as they found something.

Three weeks went by, and finally the old woman got a fax from the boat. It read: Ma'am, sorry to inform you, we found your husband dead at the bottom of the ocean. We hauled him up to the deck and attached to his butt was an oyster and inside it was a pearl worth $50,000... please advise.

The old woman faxed back: Send me the pearl and re-bait the trap.

For Over The Hill.

You're No Longer A Kid When...

1. You're asleep, but others worry that you're dead.
2. You can live without sex but not without glasses.
3. Your back goes out more than you do.
4. You quit trying to hold your stomach in, no matter who walks into the room.
5. You buy a compass for the dash of your car.
6. You are proud of your lawn mower.
7. Your best friend is dating someone half his age and isn't breaking any laws.
8. Your arms are almost too short to read the newspaper.
9. You sing along with the elevator music.
10. You would rather go to work than stay home sick.
11. You constantly talk about the price of gasoline.
12. You enjoy hearing about other people's operations.
13. You consider coffee one of the most important things in life.
14. You no longer think of speed limits as a challenge.
15. Neighbors borrow your tools.
16. People call at 9 p.m. and ask, "Did I wake you?"

For Over The Hill

17. You have a dream about prunes.
18. You answer a question with, "Because I said so!"
19. You send money to PBS.
20. The end of your tie doesn't come anywhere near the top of your pants.
21. You take a metal detector to the beach.
22. You wear black socks with sandals.
23. You can't remember the last time you laid on the floor to watch TV.
24. Your ears are hairier than your head.
25. You talk about "good grass" and you're referring to someone's lawn.
26. You get into a heated argument about pension plans.
27. You got cable for the weather channel. ("Old Folks MTV")
28. You can go bowling without drinking.
29. You have a party and the neighbors don't even realize it.
30. People give you this list.

For Over The Hill.

Getting Older

Dear family:

I have become a little older since I saw you last, and a few changes have come into my life since then. Frankly, I have become a frivolous old gal. I am seeing five gentlemen everyday. As soon as I wake up, Will Power helps me get out of bed. Then I go to see John. Then Charlie Horse comes along, and when he is here he takes a lot of my time and attention. When he leaves, Arthur Ritis shows up and stays the rest of the day. He doesn't like to stay in one place very long, so he takes me from joint to joint. After such a busy day, I'm really tired and glad to go to bed with Ben Gay. What a life. Oh yes, I'm also flirting with Al Zymer.

Love, Grandma

P.S. The preacher came to call the other day. He said at my age I should be thinking of the hereafter. I told him, "Oh, I do it frequently. No matter where I am, in the parlor, upstairs, in the kitchen, or down in the basement, I ask myself, "Now, what am I here after?"

Retirement In The Eyes Of A Child

After Christmas break from school, a teacher asked her young pupils to write how they spent the holidays. One child wrote the following…

We always spend the holidays with Grandma and Grandpa. They used to live here in a big brick house, but Grandpa got retarded and they moved to Arizona. Now they live in a place with a lot of other retarded people.

They live in a tin box and have rocks painted green to look like grass. They ride around on big tricycles and wear name tags because they don't know who they are anymore.

They go to a building called a wrecked center, but they must have got it fixed, because it is all right now. They play games and do exercises there, but they don't do them very well. There is a swimming pool too, but they all jump up and down in it with their hats on. I guess they don't know how to swim.

At their gate, there is a doll house with a little old man sitting in it. He watches all day so nobody can escape. Sometimes they sneak out. Then they go cruising in their golf carts.

My Grandma used to bake cookies and stuff, but I guess she forgot how. Nobody there cooks, they just eat out. And they eat the same thing every night - Early Birds.

Some of the people can't get past the man in the doll house to go out. So the ones who do get out bring food back to the wrecked center and call it pot luck.

My Grandma says Grandpa worked all his life to earn his retardment and says I should work hard so I can be retarded some day too. When I earn my retardment I want to be the man in the doll house. Then I will let people out so they can visit their grandchildren .

For Over The Hill

Top 25 Signs That You've Already Grown Up

1. Your potted plants stay alive.
2. Fooling around in a twinsized bed is absurd.
3. You keep more food than beer in the fridge.
4. 6:00 AM is when you get up, not when you go to sleep.
5. You hear your favorite song on an elevator.
6. You carry an umbrella. You watch the Weather Channel.
7. Your friends marry and divorce instead of hookup and breakup.
8. You go from 130 days of vacation time to 7.
9. Jeans and a sweater no longer qualify as 'dressed up'.
10. You're the one calling the police because those darn kids next door don't know how to turn down the stereo.
11. Older relatives feel comfortable telling sex jokes around you.
12. You don't know what time Taco Bell closes anymore.
13. Your car insurance goes down and your car payments go up.
14. You feed your dog Science Diet instead of McDonald's.
15. Sleeping on the couch makes your back hurt.
16. You no longer take naps from noon to 6 p.m.

For Over The Hill

17. Dinner and a movie = The whole date instead of the beginning of one.

18. MTV News is no longer your primary source for information.

19. You go to the drugstore for Ibuprofen and antacids, not condoms and pregnancy tests.

20. A $4.00 bottle of wine is no longer 'pretty good stuff.'

21. You actually eat breakfast foods at breakfast time.

22. Grocery lists are longer than macaroni & cheese, diet Pepsi & Ho-Ho's.

23. "I just can't drink the way I used to" replaces "I'm never going to drink that much again."

24. Over 90% of the time you spend in front of a computer is for real work.

25. You don't drink at home to save money before going to a bar.

For Over The Hill.

The New Boots

Sam and Bessie are senior citizens. Sam always wanted an expensive pair of alligator cowboy boots. Seeing some on sale one day, he buys a pair and wears them home, asking Bessie, "So, do you notice anything different about me?"

"What's different? It's the same shirt you wore yesterday and the same pants."

Frustrated, Sam goes into the bathroom, undresses and comes out completely naked, wearing only his new boots. Again he says, "Bessie, do you notice anything different?"

"What's different, Sam? It's hanging down today, it was hanging down yesterday, and it will be hanging down tomorrow."

Angrily, Sam yells, "Do you know why it's hanging down? 'Cause it's looking at my new boots!"

Bessie replies, "You shoulda bought a hat."

For Over The Hill

Slow Dance

Have you ever watched kids on a merry-go-round?
Or listened to the rain slapping on the ground?
Ever followed a butterfly's erratic flight?
Or gazed at the sun into the fading night?
You better slow down. Don't dance so fast.
Time is short. The music won't last.

Do you run through each day on the fly?
When you ask "How are you?"
Do you hear the reply?
When the day is done do you lie in your bed
with the next hundred chores running through your head?
You'd better slow down. Don't dance so fast.
Time is short. The music won't last.

Ever told your child, "we'll do it tomorrow?"
And in your haste, not see his sorrow?
Ever lost touch, let a good friendship die
cause you never had time to call and say "Hi"?
You'd better slow down. Don't dance so fast.
Time is short. The music won't last.

When you run so fast to get somewhere
you miss half the fun of getting there.
When you worry and hurry through your
day, it is like an unopened gift....
Thrown away. Life is not a race.
Do take it slower, hear the music,
before the song is over.

For Over The Hill.

How Do You Live Your Dash?

I read of a man who stood to speak at the funeral of a friend he referred to the dates on her tombstone from the beginning... to the end.

He noted that first came her date of birth and spoke the following date with tears, but he said what mattered most of all was the dash between those years. (1934 -1998)

For that dash represents all the time that she spent alive on earth... and now only those who loved her know what that little line is worth.

For it matters not, how much we own; the cars... the house... the cash. What matters is how we live and love and how we spend our dash.

So think about this long and hard... are there things you'd like to change? For you never know how much time is left, that can still be rearranged.

If we could just slow down enough to consider what's true and real, and always try to understand the way other people feel.

And be less quick to anger, and show appreciation more and love the people in our lives like we've never loved before.

If we treat each other with respect, and more often wear a smile... remembering that this special dash might only last a little while.

So, when your eulogy's being read with your life's actions to rehash... would you be proud of the things they say about how you spent your dash?

For Parents

Daddy's Day

Her hair up in a pony tail, her favorite dress tied with a bow, today was Daddy's Day at school, and she couldn't wait to go. But her mommy tried to tell her that she probably should stay home. Why the kids might not understand if she went to school alone.

But she was not afraid; she knew just what to say what to tell her classmates, on this Daddy's Day. But still her mother worried for her to face this day alone And that was why once again, she tried to keep her daughter home.

But the little girl went to school, eager to tell them all about a dad she never sees, a dad who never calls. There were daddies along the wall in back, for everyone to meet. Children squirming impatiently, anxious in their seats.

One by one the teacher called a student from the class to introduce his daddy as seconds slowly passed. At last the teacher called her name. Every child turned to stare. Each of them was searching for a man who wasn't there.

"Where's her daddy at?" she heard a boy call out .
"She probably doesn't have one," another student dared to shout.

And from somewhere near the back, she heard a daddy say "Looks like another deadbeat dad, too busy to waste his day."

Continued on next page

For Parents

Continued from previous page

The words did not offend her as she smiled at her friends and looked back at her teacher who told her to begin. With hands behind her back, slowly she began to speak and out from the mouth of a child came words incredibly unique.

"My Daddy couldn't be here because he lives so far away but I know he wishes he could be with me on this day. And though you cannot meet him, I wanted you to know all about my daddy, and how much he loves me so. He loved to tell me stories, he taught me to ride my bike. He surprised me with pink roses, and taught me to fly a kite.

We used to share fudge sundaes, and ice cream in a cone and though you cannot see him, I'm not standing all alone cause my daddy's always with me, even though we are apart. I know because he told me, he'll forever be here in my heart".

With that her little hand reached up and lay across her chest. Feeling her own heartbeat beneath her favorite dress and from somewhere in the crowd of dads, her mother stood in tears proudly watching her daughter, who was wise beyond her years. For she stood up for the love of a man not in her life doing what was best for her, doing what was right.

And when she dropped her hand back down, staring straight into the crowd, she finished with a voice so soft, but its message clear and loud.

68

For Parents

"I love my daddy very much; he's my shining star. And if he could he'd be here, but heaven's just too far,. But sometimes when I close my eyes, it's like he never went away." And then she closed her eyes, and saw him there that day.

To her mother's amazement, she witnessed with surprise a room full of daddies and children, all starting to close their eyes. Who knows what they saw before them, who knows what they felt inside perhaps for merely a second, they saw him at her side.

"I know you're with me Daddy," to the silence she called out. What happened next made believers of those once filled with doubt. Not one in that room could explain it, for each of their eyes had been closed But there placed on her desktop, was a beautiful fragrant pink rose

And a child was blessed, if only a moment, by the love of her shining bright star and given the gift of believing, that heaven is never too far.

To all the little girls and boys whose moms and dads were lost in the September 11th tragedy our prayers are with you all.

For Parents

Vaseline

A little boy came down for breakfast one morning and asked his grandma, "Where's Mom and Dad?" and she replied, "They're up in bed."

The little boy started to giggle and ate his breakfast and went out to play. Then he came back in for lunch and asked his grandma "Where's Mom and Dad?" And she replied, "They're still up in bed."

Again the little boy started to giggle and he ate his lunch and went out to play. Then the little boy came in for dinner and once again he asked his grandma "Where's Mom and dad?" And his grandmother replied, "They're still up in bed."

The little boy started to laugh and his grandmother asked, "What gives? Every time I tell you they're still up in bed you start to laugh! What is going on here?" The little boy replied, "Well last night daddy came into my bedroom and asked me for the Vaseline and I gave him super glue."

—— 🐌 ——

A mother was telling her little girl what her own childhood was like: "We used to skate outside on a pond. I had a swing made from a tire; it hung from a tree in our front yard. We rode our pony. We picked wild raspberries in the woods." The little girl was wide-eyed, taking this in. At last she said, "I sure wish I'd gotten to know you sooner!"

For Parents

Kid Stories ....

After putting her children to bed, a mother changed into old slacks and a droopy blouse and proceeded to wash her hair. As she heard the children getting more and more rambunctious, her patience grew thin. At last she threw a towel around her head and stormed into their room, putting them back to bed with stern warnings. As she left the room, she heard her three-year-old say with a trembling voice, "Who was THAT?"

My grandson was visiting one day when he asked, "Grandma, do you know how you and God are alike?" I mentally polished my halo while I asked, "No, how are we alike?" "You're both old," he replied.

A little girl was diligently pounding away on her father's word processor. She told him she was writing a story. "What's it about?" he asked. "I don't know," she replied. "I can't read."

I didn't know if my granddaughter had learned her colors yet, so I decided to test her. I would point out something and ask what color it was. She would tell me, and always she was correct. But, it was fun for me, so I continued. At last she headed for the door, saying sagely, "Grandma, I think you should try to figure out some of these yourself!"

Continued on next page

For Parents

Continued from previous page

A Sunday school class was studying the Ten Commandments. They were ready to discuss the last one. The teacher asked if anyone could tell her what it was. Susie raised her hand, stood tall, and quoted, "Thou shall not take the covers off thy neighbor's wife."

———— 🐌 ————

Our five-year-old son Mark couldn't wait to tell his father about the movie we had watched on television, *20,000 Leagues Under the Sea*. The scenes with the submarine and the giant octopus had kept him wide-eyed. In the middle of the telling, my husband interrupted Mark, "What caused the submarine to sink?" With a look of incredulity Mark replied, "Dad, it was the 20,000 leaks!"

———— 🐌 ————

When my grandson Billy and I entered our vacation cabin, we kept the lights off until we were inside to keep from attracting pesky insects. Still, a few fireflies followed us in. Noticing them before I did, Billy whispered, "It's no use, Grandpa. The mosquitoes are coming after us with flashlights."

———— 🐌 ————

A second grader came home from school and said to her mother, "Mom, guess what? We learned how to make babies today."

The mother, more than a little surprised, tried to keep her cool. "That's interesting," she said. "How do you make babies?"

"It's simple," replied the girl. "You just change 'y' to 'i' and add 'es'."

The Storm

A little girl walked daily to and from school. Though the weather that morning was questionable and clouds were forming, she made her daily trek to the elementary school. As the thunderstorm progressed, the winds whipped up, along with thunder and lightening.

The mother of the little girl felt concerned that her daughter would be frightened as she walked home from school, and she herself feared that the electrical storm might harm her child. Following the roar of thunder, lightning, like a flaming sword, would cut through the sky. Full of concern, the mother quickly got into her car and drove along the route to her child's school. As she did so, she saw her little girl walking along, but at each flash of lightning, the child would stop, look and smile. Another and another flash of lightning were to follow quickly, each with the little girl stopping, looking at the streak of light and smiling. Finally, the mother called her over to the car and asked, "What are you doing?" The child answered, "God just keeps taking pictures of me."

For Parents

Dear God - Prayers of Youngsters

Dear GOD, Instead of letting people die and having to make new ones, why don't You just keep the ones You have?

Dear GOD, Maybe Cain and Abel would not kill each other so much if they had their own rooms. It worked with my brother.

Dear GOD, If You watch me in church on Sunday, I'll show you my new shoes.

Dear GOD, I bet it is very hard for You to love all of everybody in the whole world. There are only 4 people in our family and I can never do it.

Dear GOD, In school they told us what You do. Who does it when You are on vacation?

Dear GOD, Are You really invisible or is it just a trick?

Dear GOD, Is it true my father won't get in Heaven if he uses his bowling words in the house?

Dear GOD, Who draws the lines around the countries?

Dear GOD, I went to this wedding and they kissed right in church. Is that okay?

Dear GOD, What does it mean You are a Jealous God? I thought You had everything.

For Parents

Dear GOD, did You really mean "Do unto others as they do unto you"? Because if You did, then I'm going to fix my brother.

Dear GOD, thank you for the baby brother, but what I prayed for was a puppy.

Dear GOD, it rained for our whole vacation and is my father mad! He said some things about You that people are not supposed to say, but I hope You will not hurt him anyway. Your friend, (But I am not going to tell You who I am)

Dear GOD, why is Sunday school on Sunday? I thought it was supposed to be our day of rest.

Dear GOD, please send me a pony. I never asked for anything before. You can look it up.

Dear GOD, if we come back as something - Please don't let me be Jennifer Horton because I hate her.

Dear GOD, if you give me a genie like Aladdin, I will give You anything You want, except my money or my chess set.

Dear GOD, my brother is a rat. You should give him a tail.

Dear GOD, I want to be just like my Daddy when I get big, but not with so much hair all over.

Continued on next page

For Parents

Continued from previous page

Dear GOD, you don't have to worry about me. I always look both ways.

Dear GOD, I think the stapler is one of your greatest inventions.

Dear GOD, of all the people who work for You I like Noah and David the best.

Dear GOD, I would like to live 900 years like the guy in the Bible.

Dear GOD, we read Thomas Edison made light. But in Sunday school they said You did it. So I bet he stole your idea.

Dear GOD, I do not think anybody could be a better GOD. Well, I just want You to know but I am not just saying that because You are GOD already.

Dear GOD, I didn't think orange went with purple until I saw the sunset you made on Tuesday. That was cool.

—— ᓚᘏᗢ ——

A psychiatrist is a person who will give you expensive answers that your wife will give you for free.

For Professionals

The Engineer

So, the engineer reported to the gates of hell and was admitted. Soon, the engineer became dissatisfied with the level of comfort in hell, and started designing and building improvements. Soon, Hell's got air conditioning, flush toilets, cable TV, Internet access, swimming pools, a brewery and escalators, and the engineer became a pretty popular guy. Eventually, an audit disclosed serious discrepancies in Hell's environment.

God called Satan up on the telephone and asked, "So, how's it going down there?"

Satan replied, "Hey, things are going great. We've got air conditioning and flush toilets and escalators. We've acquired all kinds of amenities, and there's no telling what this engineer is going to come up with next."

God replied, "What??? You've got an engineer? That's a mistake. He should never have gotten down there; send him up here!"

Satan said, "No way. I like having an engineer on the staff, and I'm keeping him."

God said, "Send him back up here or I'll sue."

Satan laughed uproariously and answered, "Yeah, right. And just where are YOU going to get a lawyer?"

For Professionals

Courtroom Humor

A defense attorney was cross-examining a police officer during a felony trial - it went like this:

Q. Officer, did you see my client fleeing the scene?

A. No sir, but I subsequently observed a person matching the description of the offender running several blocks away.

Q. Officer, who provided this description?

A. The officer who responded to the scene.

Q. A fellow officer provided the description of this so-called offender. Do you trust your fellow officers?

A. Yes sir, with my life.

Q. With your life? Let me ask you this then officer - do you have a locker room in the police station - a room where you change your clothes in preparation for your daily duties?

A. Yes sir, we do.

Q. And do you have a locker in that room?

A. Yes sir, I do.

Q. And do you have a lock on your locker?

A. Yes sir.

Q. Now why is it, officer, if you trust your fellow officers with your life, that you find it necessary to lock your locker in a room you share with those same officers?

A. You see sir, we share the building with a court complex, and sometimes lawyers have been known to walk through that room.

With that, the courtroom erupted in laughter, and a prompt recess was called. The officer on the stand has been nominated for this year's "Best comeback" line and we think he'll win.

For Professionals

Medical Humor

A man comes into the ER and yells "My wife's going to have her baby in the cab!" The ER physician grabs his stuff, rushes out to the cab, lifts the lady's dress, and begins to take off her underwear. Suddenly he notices that there are several cabs, and he's in the wrong one.

———   ଽ⚫   ———

A nurse at the beginning of the shift places her stethoscope on an elderly and slightly deaf female patient's anterior chest wall. "Big breaths," instructed the nurse. "Yes, they used to be," replied the patient.

———   ଽ⚫   ———

One day I had to be the bearer of bad news when I told a wife that her husband had died of a massive myocardial infarction. Not more than five minutes later, I heard her reporting to the rest of the family that he had died of a "massive internal fart."

———   ଽ⚫   ———

I was performing a complete physical, including the visual acuity test. I placed the patient twenty feet from the chart and began, "Cover your right eye with your hand." He read the 20/20 line perfectly. "Now your left." Again, a flawless read. "Now both," I requested. There was silence. He couldn't even read the large E on the top line. I turned and discovered that he had done exactly what I had asked; he was standing there with both his eyes covered. I was laughing too hard to finish the exam.

Continued on next page

For Professionals

Continued from previous page

A nurses' aide was helping a patient into the bathroom when the patient exclaimed, "You're not coming in here with me. This is a one-seater!"

——— ❧ ———

During a patient's two week follow-up appointment with his cardiologist, he informed his doctor that he was having trouble with one of his medications. "Which one?" Asked the doctor.

"The patch. The nurse told me to put on a new one every six hours and now I'm running out of places to put it!" The doctor had him quickly undress and discovered what he hoped he wouldn't see.... Yes, the man had over fifty patches on his body!

Now the instructions include removal of the old patch before applying a new one.

——— ❧ ———

While acquainting myself with a new elderly patient, I asked, "How long have you been bedridden?" After a look of complete confusion she answered, "Why, not for about twenty years-when my husband was alive."

For Professionals

Unusual Taste

A nurse caring for a woman from Kentucky asked, "So how's your breakfast this morning?" "It's very good, except for the Kentucky Jelly. I can't seem to get used to the taste," the patient replied. The nurse asked to see the jelly and the woman produced a foil packet labeled "KY Jelly."

A Brunette, a Redhead and a Blonde escape a burning building by climbing to the roof. Firemen are on the street below, holding a blanket for them to jump in. The firemen yell to the Brunette, "Jump! Jump! It's your only chance to survive!" The Brunette jumps and SWISH! The firemen yank the blanket away. The Brunette slams into the sidewalk like a tomato.

"C'mon! Jump! You gotta jump!" say the firemen to the Redhead. "Oh no! You're gonna pull the blanket away!" says the Redhead.

"No! It's Brunettes we can't stand! We're OK with Redheads!"

"OK," says the Redhead, and she jumps. SWISH! The firemen yank the blanket away, and the lady is flattened on the pavement like a pancake.

Finally, the Blonde steps to the edge of the roof. Again, the firemen yell, "Jump! You have to jump!"

"No way! You're just gonna pull the blanket away!" yells the Blonde.

"No! Really! You have to jump! We won't pull the blanket away!"

"Look," the Blonde says. "Nothing you say is gonna convince me that you're not gonna pull the blanket away! So what I want you to do is put the blanket down, and back away from it..."

For Professionals

Country Folk's Medical Terms

Benign	What you be after you be eight.
Bacteria	Back door to cafeteria.
Barium	What doctors do when patients die.
Cesarean Section	A neighborhood in Rome.
Catscan	Searching for Kitty.
Cauterize	Made eye contact with her.
Colic	A sheep dog.
Coma	A punctuation mark.
Dilate	To live long.
Enema	Not a friend.
Fibula	A small lie.
Genital	Non-Jewish person.
G.I.Series	World Series of military baseball.
Hangnail	What you hang your coat on.
Impotent	Distinguished, well-known.
Labor Pain	Getting hurt at work.
Morbid	A higher offer than I bid.
Node	I knew it.
Outpatient	A person who has fainted.
Pap Smear	A fatherhood test.
Pelvis	Second cousin to Elvis.
Post Operative	A letter carrier.
Recovery Room	Place to do upholstery.
Rectum	Damn near killed him.
Secretion	Hiding something.
Seizure	Roman emperor.
Tumor	More than one.
Urine	Opposite of mine.
Varicose	Near by/close by.

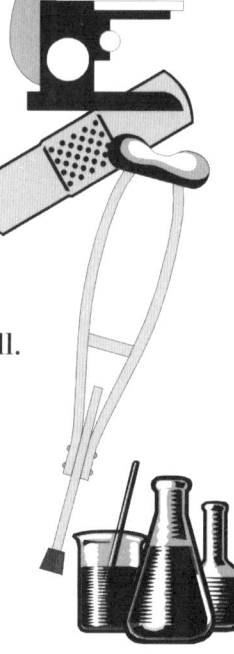

For Professionals

Job Challenges

Take heart, anyone among you who believe you are Technologically Challenged, you "ain't seen nuthin'" yet. This is an excerpt from a Wall Street Journal article:

1. Compaq is considering changing the command "Press Any Key" to "Press Return Key" because of the flood of calls asking where the "Any" key is.

2. AST technical support had a caller complaining that her mouse was hard to control with the dust cover on. The cover turned out to be the plastic bag the mouse was packaged in.

3. Another AST customer was asked to send a copy of her defective diskettes. A few days later a letter arrived from the customer along with photocopies of the floppies.

4. A Dell technician advised his customer to put his troubled floppy back in the drive and close the door. The customer asked the tech to hold on and was heard putting the phone down, getting up and crossing the room to close the door to his room.

5. Another Dell customer called to say he couldn't get his computer to fax anything. After 40 minutes of troubleshooting, the technician discovered the man was trying to fax a piece of paper by holding it in front of the monitor screen and hitting the "send" key.

6. Yet another Dell customer called to complain that his keyboard no longer worked. He had cleaned it by filling up his tub with soap and water and soaking the keyboard removing all the keys and washing them individually.

Continued on next page

For Professionals

Continued from previous page

7. A Dell technician received a call from a customer who was enraged because his computer had told him he was "bad and an invalid," The tech explained that the computer's "bad command" and "invalid" response shouldn't be taken personally.

8. A confused caller to IBM was having trouble printing documents. He told the technician that the computer had said it "couldn't find printer." The user had also tried turning the computer screen to face the printer-but that his computer still couldn't "see" the printer.

9. An exasperated caller to Dell Computer Tech Support couldn't get her new Dell Computer to turn on. After ensuring the computer was plugged in, the technician asked her what happened when she pushed the power button. Her response, "I pushed and pushed on this foot pedal and nothing happens." The "foot pedal" turned out to be the computer's mouse.

10. Another customer called Compaq tech support to say her brand-new computer wouldn't work. She said she unpacked the unit, plugged it in and sat there for 20 minutes waiting for something to happen. When asked what happened when she pressed the power switch, she asked, "What power switch?"

11. Another IBM customer had trouble installing software and rang for support. "I put in the first disk, and that was OK. It said to put in the second disk, and had some problems with the disk. When it said to put in the third disk, I couldn't even fit it in..." The user hadn't realized that "Insert Disk 2" meant to remove Disk 1 first.

For Professionals

12. In a similar incident, a customer had followed the instructions for installing software. The instructions said to remove the disk from its cover and insert into the drive. The user had physically removed the casing of the disk and wondered why there were problems.

13. A woman called the Canon help desk with a problem with her printer. The tech asked her if she was running it under "Windows." The woman responded, "No, my desk is next to the door. But that is a good point. The man sitting in the cubicle next to me is under a window and his printer is working fine."

14. TECH SUPPORT: "O.K. Bob, let's press the control and escape keys at the same time. That brings up a task list in the middle of the screen. Now type the letter "P" to bring up the Program Manager." CUSTOMER: "I don't have a 'P'".
    TECH SUPPORT: "On your keyboard, Bob."
    CUSTOMER: "What do you mean?"
    TECH SUPPORT: "'P' on your keyboard, Bob."
    CUSTOMER: "I'm not going to do that!"

15. Overheard in a computer shop:
    CUSTOMER: "I'd like a mouse mat, please."
    SALESPERSON: "Certainly, Sir. We've got a large variety."
    CUSTOMER: "But will they be compatible with my computer?"

16. I once received a fax with a note on the bottom to fax the document back to the sender when I finished with it, because he needed to keep it.

For Professionals.

Things Not To Say To An Officer

1. I can't reach my license unless you hold my beer. (OK in Texas)

2. Sorry, Officer, I didn't realize my radar detector wasn't plugged in.

3. Aren't you the guy from the Village People?

4. Hey, you must've been doing about 125 mph to keep up with me. Good job!

5. Are you Andy or Barney?

6. I thought you had to be in relatively good physical condition to be a police officer.

7. You're not gonna check the trunk, are you?

8. I pay your salary!

9. Man, Officer! That's terrific. The last officer only gave me a warning, too!

10. Do you know why you pulled me over? Okay, just so one of us does.

11. I was trying to keep up with traffic. Yes, I know there are no other cars around. That's how far ahead of me they are.

12. When the Officer says "Son....Your eyes look red, have you been drinking?" You probably shouldn't respond with, "Officer your eyes look glazed, have you been eating doughnuts?"

For Rednecks

North vs South

If you are from the northern states and planning on visiting or moving to the South, there are a few things you should know that will help you adapt to the difference in life-styles:

The North has sun dried toe-mah-toes, The South has 'mater samiches.

The North has coffeehouses, The South has Waffle Houses.

The North has dating services, The South has family reunions.

The North has switchblade knives, The South has Lee Press-on Nails.

The North has double last names, The South has double first names.

The North has Ted Kennedy, The South has Jesse Helms.

The North has an ambulance, The South has an amalance.

The North has the Mafia, The South has the Klan.

The North has Indy car races, The South has stock car races.

The North has Cream of Wheat, The South has grits.

The North has green salads, The South has collard greens.

The North has lobsters, The South has craw dads.

The North has the rust belt, The South has the Bible Belt.

The North has Barney Frank, The South has Bill Clinton.

Continued on next page

Continued from previous page

If you run your car into a ditch, don't panic. Four men in a four-wheel drive pickup truck with a tow chain will be along shortly. Don't try to help them, just stay out of their way. This is what they live for.

Don't be surprised to find movie rentals and bait in the same store. Don't buy food at this store.

Remember, "ya'll" is singular, "all ya'll" is plural, and "all ya'll's" is plural possessive.

Get used to hearing "You ain't from around here, are ya?"

You may hear a Southerner say "Ought'" to a dog or child. This is short for "Ya'll ought not do that" and is the equivalent of saying "No".

Don't be worried at not understanding what people are saying. They can't understand you either.

The first Southern expression to creep into a transplanted Northerner's vocabulary is the adjective "big ol," as in "big ol truck" or "big ol boy."

Most Northerners begin their Southern influenced dialect this way. All of them are in denial about it.

The proper pronunciation you learned in school is no longer proper.

Be advised that 'He needed killin' is a valid defense here.

For Rednecks

If you hear a Southerner exclaim, "Hey, ya'll, watch this," stay out of the way. These are likely to be the last words he'll ever say.

If there is the prediction of the slightest chance of even the smallest accumulation of snow, your presence is required at the local grocery store. It doesn't matter whether you need anything or not. You just have to go there.

When you come upon a person driving 15 mph down the middle of the road, remember that most folks learn to drive on a John Deere, and that this is the proper speed and position for that vehicle.

Do not be surprised to find that 10-year-olds own their own shotguns, they are proficient marksmen, and their mammas taught them how to aim.

In the South, we have found that the best way to grow a lush, green lawn is to pour gravel on it and call it a driveway.

If you do settle in the South and bear children, don't think we will accept them as Southerners. After all, if the cat had kittens in the oven, we wouldn't call em biscuits.

For Rednecks

Red-Neck Valentine's Love Poem

Collards is green my dog's name is Blue
and I'm so lucky to have a sweet thang like you.

Yore hair is like cornsilk a-flapping in the breeze
Softer than Blue's and without all them fleas.

You move like the bass, which excite me in May.
You ain't got no scales but I luv you anyway.

Yo're as satisfy'n as okry jist a-fry'n in the pan.
Yo're as fragrant as "snuff" right out of the can.

You have som'a yore teeth, for which I am proud;
I hold my head high when we're in a crowd.

On special occasions, when you shave under yore arms,
well, I'm in hawg heaven, and awed by yore charms.

Still them fellers at work, they all want to know,
what I did to deserve such a purdy, young doe.

Like a good roll of duct tape yo're there fer yore man,
to patch up life's troubles and fix what you can.
Yo're as cute as a junebug a-buzzin' overhead.
You ain't mean like those far ants I found in my bed.

Cut from the best cloth like a plaid flannel shirt,
you spark up my life more than a fresh load of dirt.

For Rednecks

When you hold me real tight like a padded gunrack,
my life is complete; Ain't nuttin' I lack.

Yore complexion, it's perfection, like the best vinyl sidin'.
Despite all the years, yore age, it keeps hidin'.

Me 'n' you's like a Moon Pie with a RC cold drank,
we go together like a skunk goes with stank.

Some men, they buy chocolate for Valentine's Day;
They git it at Wal-Mart, it's romantic that way.

Some men git roses on that special day
from the cooler at Kroger. "That's impressive," I say.

Some men buy fine diamonds from a flea market booth.
"Diamonds are forever," they explain, suave and couth.

But for this man, honey, these won't do.
Cause yo're too special, you sweet thang you.

I got you a gift, without taste nor odor,
more useful than diamonds...
It's a new trollin' motor!!

For Rednecks

Southern Sayings

1. "Well, butter my butt and call me a biscuit."
2. "It's been hotter'n a goat's butt in a pepper patch."
3. "He fell out of the ugly tree and hit every branch on the way down."
4. "Have a cup of coffee, it's already been 'saucered and blowed.'"
5. "She's so stuck up, she'd drown in a rainstorm."
6. "It's so dry, the trees are bribing the dogs."
7. "My cow died last night so I don't need your bull."
8. "Don't pee down my back and tell me it's raining."
9. "He's as country as Cornflakes."
10. "This is gooder'n grits."
11. "Busier than a cat covering crap on a marble floor."
12. "If things get any better, I may have to hire someone to help me enjoy it."
13. "Well knock me down and steal muh teeth!"
14. "I'll slap you so hard, your clothes will be outta style."
15. "This'll jar your preserves."
16. "Cute as a sack full of puppies."
17. Wintery roads are said to be "slicker than otter snot."
18. If something is hard to do, it's "like trying to herd cats."
19. "She's uglier than homemade soap."
20. "You're uglier than a lard bucket full of armpits."
21. I'll slap you so much, you'll think yur surrounded.

You Might Be A Redneck If:

1. If you have a complete set of salad bowls and they all say Cool Whip on the side.
2. If the biggest city you've ever been to is Wal-Mart.
3. If your working TV sits on top of your non-working TV.
4. If you thought the Unibomber was a wrestler.
5. If you've ever used your ironing board as a buffet table.
6. If you think a quarter horse is that ride in front of K-Mart.
7. If your neighbors think you're a detective because a cop always brings you home.
8. If a tornado hits your neighborhood and does a $100,000 worth improvement.
9. If you've ever used a toilet brush as a back scratcher.
10. If you've ever asked the preacher "How's it hangin?"
11. If you missed 5th grade graduation because you had jury duty.
12. If you think fast food is hitting a deer at 65 mph.
13. If somebody tells you that you've got something in your teeth and you take them out to see what it is.
14. If you've ever stared at a can of orange juice because it said concentrate.

For Rednecks

Dear Redneck Son;

I'm writing this letter slow because I know you can't read fast. We don't live where we did when you left home. Your dad read in the newspaper that most accidents happen within 2 miles from your home, so we moved. I won't be able to send you the address because the last Georgia family that lived here took the house numbers when they moved so that they wouldn't have to change their address.

This place is really nice. It even has a washing machine. I'm not sure it works so well though: last week I put a load in and pulled the chain and haven't seen them since.

The weather isn't bad here. It only rained twice last week: the first time for three days and the second time for four days.

About that coat you wanted me to send you, your Uncle Stanley said it would be too heavy to send in the mail with the buttons on, so we cut them off and put them in the pockets.

John locked his keys in the car yesterday. We were really worried because it took him two hours to get me and your father out.

Your sister had a baby this morning; but I haven't found out what it is yet so I don't know if your an aunt or an uncle.

Uncle Ted fell in a whiskey vat last week. Some men tried to pull him out, but he fought them off playfully and drowned. We had him cremated and he burned for three days.

Three of your friends went off a bridge in a pick-up truck. Ralph was driving. He rolled down the window and swam to safety. Your other two friends were in back. They drowned because they couldn't get the tailgate down.

There isn't much more news at this time. Nothing much has happened.
Love, Mom

P.S. I was going to send you some money but the envelope was already sealed.

Redneck Birth

In the back woods of Kentucky, the redneck's wife went into labor in the middle of the night, and the doctor was called out to assist in the delivery. Since there was no electricity, the doctor handed the father-to-be a lantern and said, "Here, you hold this high so I can see what I am doing."

Soon, a baby boy was brought into the world.

"Whoa there," said the doctor. "Don't be in a rush to put the lantern down....I think there's yet another one to come." Sure enough, within minutes he had delivered a baby girl.

"No, no, don't be in a great hurry to put down that lantern... It seems there's yet another one to come."

Sure enough, within minutes he had delivered another baby girl.

"No, no, don't be in a great hurry to put down that lantern.... It seems there's yet another one in there!" cried the doctor.

The redneck scratched his head in bewilderment, and asked the doctor....

"Do you think it's the light that's attractin' 'em?"

Why do drivers education classes in Redneck schools use the car only on Mondays, Wednesdays, and Fridays? Because on Tuesday and Thursday, the sex ed class uses it.

For Rednecks

A Visit To The Mall

A redneck family from the hills was visiting the city and they were in a mall for the first time in their lives. The father and son were strolling around while the wife shopped. They were amazed by almost everything they saw, but especially by two shiny, silver walls that could move apart and then slide back together again.

The boy asked, "Paw, What's 'at?" The father (never having seen an elevator) responded, "Son, I dunno. I ain't never seen anything like that in my entire life, I ain't got no idea'r what it is."

While the boy and his father were watching with amazement, a fat old lady in a wheel chair rolled up to the moving walls and pressed a button. The walls opened and the lady rolled between them into a small room. The walls closed and the boy and his father watched the small circular numbers above the walls light up sequentially. They continued to watch until it reached the last number and then the numbers began to light in the reverse order. Then the walls opened up again and a gorgeous, voluptuous 24-year-old blonde woman stepped out. The father, not taking his eyes off the young woman, said quietly to his son, "Boy, go git yo Momma...."

For Relationships

Do Unto Others..

A frail old man went to live with his son, daughter-in-law and 4-year-old grandson. The old man's hands trembled, his eyesight blurred, and his step faltered.

The family ate together at the table, but the elderly grandfather's shaky hands and failing sight made eating difficult. Peas rolled off the spoon onto the floor. When he grasped the glass, milk spilled on the tablecloth.

The son and daughter-in-law became irritated with the mess. "We must do something with Grandpa," said the son. "I have had enough of spilled milk, noisy eating, and food on the floor." So the husband and the wife set a small table in the corner. There Grandpa ate alone while the rest of the family enjoyed their dinner.

Since Grandpa had broken a dish or two, his food was served in a wooden bowl. When the family glanced in Grandpa's direction, sometimes he had a tear in his eye as he sat alone.

Still the only words the couple had for him were sharp admonitions when he dropped his fork or spilled food. The 4-year-old watched it all in silence.

One evening before supper, the father noticed his son playing with wood scraps on the floor. He asked the child sweetly, "What are you making?"

Continued on next page

For Relationship

Continued from previous page

Just as sweetly the boy responded, "Oh, I am making a little wooden bowl for you and Mom to eat your food when I grow up." The 4-year-old smiled and went on with his work.

The words so struck the parents that they were speechless. Then tears started to stream down their cheeks. Though no words were spoken, both knew what must be done.

That evening the husband took the Grandfather's hand and gently led him to the family table. For the remainder of his days he ate every meal with the family.

For some reason, neither the husband nor wife seemed to care any longer when a fork dropped, milk spilled, or the tablecloth soiled.

Children are remarkably perceptive. Their eyes ever observe, their ears ever listen, and their minds ever process the messages they absorb.

If they see us patiently provide a happy home atmosphere for family members, they will imitate that attitude for the rest of their lives. The wise parent realizes that every day the building blocks are being laid for the child's future.

Let's be wise builders and role models.

For Relationship

Yesterday I Met A Stranger...

Today this stranger is my friend.

Had I not taken the time to say hello, or return a smile, or shake a hand, or listen, I would not have known this person.

Yesterday would have turned into today and our chance meeting would be gone.

Yesterday I hugged someone very dear to me.

Today they are gone. And tomorrow will not bring them back.

Wouldn't it be nice if we all knew tomorrow would be here?

But this is not to be, so take the time TODAY to give a hug, a smile, an "I love you."

Regis Philbin is in bed with his wife and starts to get a little frisky. She rolls over and says "Not tonight Reg, I have a headache."

He responds "Is that your final answer?"

She says "Yes, Regis, that's my final answer!"

Regis replies, "Well in that case, I'd like to phone a friend."

For Relationship

Just For Today...

Smile at a stranger...

Listen to someone's heart...

Drop a coin where a child can find it...

Learn something new, then teach it to someone...

Tell someone you're thinking of him...

Hug a loved one...

Don't hold a grudge...

Don't be afraid to say "I'm sorry"...

Look a child in the eye and tell him how great he is...

Don't kill that spider in your house; he's just lost so show him the way out...

Look beyond the face of a person into his heart...

Make a promise, and keep it...

Call someone, for no other reason than to just say "Hi"...

Show kindness to an animal...

Stand up for what you believe in...

Smell the rain, feel the breeze, listen to the wind...

Use all your senses to their fullest...

Cherish all your TODAYS.

Today you were thought about by me.

Give this to someone special and let him know he was thought about TODAY.

For Relationship

The Importance Of Using Correct E-mail Addresses

A couple from Minneapolis decided to go to Florida for a long weekend to thaw out during one particularly icy winter. Because both had jobs, they had difficulty coordinating their travel schedules. It was decided that the husband would fly to Florida on a Thursday, and his wife would follow him the next day. Upon arriving as planned, the husband checked into the hotel. There he decided to open his laptop and send his wife an e-mail back in Minneapolis. However, he accidentally left off one letter in her address, and sent the e-mail without realizing his error. In Houston, a widow had just returned from her husband's funeral. He was a minister of many years who had been 'called home to glory' following a heart attack.

The widow checked her e-mail, expecting messages from relatives and friends. Upon reading the first message, she fainted and fell to the floor. The widow's son rushed into the room, found his mother on the floor, and saw the computer screen which read:

To: My Loving Wife
From: Your Departed Husband
Subject: I've Arrived!

I've just arrived and have been checked in. I see that everything has been prepared for your arrival tomorrow. Looking forward to seeing you then!

Hope your journey is as uneventful as mine was.

P.S. Sure is hot down here!

For Relationship

Relationship Funnies

1. Getting married is very much like going to a restaurant with friends. You order what you want, then when you see what the other person has, you wish you had ordered that.
2. At the cocktail party, one woman said to another, "Aren't you wearing your wedding ring on the wrong finger?" The other replied, "Yes I am. I married the wrong man."
3. After a quarrel, a husband said to his wife, "You know, I was a fool when I married you." She replied, "Yes, dear, but I was in love and didn't notice."
4. A lady inserted an ad in the classifieds: "Husband wanted." Next day she received a hundred letters. They all said the same thing: "You can have mine."
5. A little boy asked his father, "Daddy, how much does it cost to get married?" And the father replied, "I don't know son, I'm still paying."
6. Marriage is the triumph of imagination over intelligence. Second marriage is the triumph of hope over experience.
7. If you want your spouse to listen and pay strict attention to every word you say, talk in your sleep.
8. First guy (proudly): "My wife's an angel!" Second guy: "You're lucky; mine's still alive."
9. How do you scare a man? Sneak up behind him and start throwing rice.
10. What makes men chase women they have no intention of marrying? The same urge that makes dogs chase cars they have no intention of driving.

For Relationship

The Hateful Husband

An old man and woman were married for years, even though they hated each other. When they had a confrontation, screaming and yelling could be heard deep into the night. The old man would shout, "When I die, I will dig my way up and out of the grave and come back and haunt you for the rest of your life!"

Neighbors feared him. They believed he practiced black magic because of the many strange occurrences that took place in their neighborhood. The old man liked the fact he was feared.

To everyone's relief, he died of a heart attack when he was 68. His wife had a closed casket at the wake. After the burial, she went straight to the local bar and began to party as if there was no tomorrow.

Her neighbors, concerned for her safety, asked, "Aren't you afraid that he may indeed be able to dig his way up and out of the grave and come back and haunt you for the rest of your life?"

The wife put down her drink and said, "Let him dig. I had him buried upside down.

For Relationship

Instructions for Life & Relationships

1. Give people more than they expect and do it cheerfully.
2. Memorize your favorite poem.
3. Don't believe all you hear, spend all you have, or loaf all you want.
4. When you say, "I love you," mean it.
5. When you say, "I'm sorry," look the person in the eye.
6. Approach love and cooking with reckless abandon.
7. Believe in love at first sight.
8. Never laugh at anyone's dreams. People who don't have dreams, don't have much.
9. Love deeply and passionately. You may get hurt, but it's the only way to live life completely.
10. In disagreements, fight fairly. No name-calling.
11. Don't judge people by their relatives, or by the life they were born into.
12. Teach yourself to speak slowly but think quickly.
13. When someone asks you a question you don't want to answer, smile and ask, "Why do you want to know?"
14. Take into account that great love and great achievements involve great risk.
15. Call your mother.

For Relationship

16. Say, "Bless you" when you hear someone sneeze.
17. When you lose, don't lose the lesson.
18. Follow the three R's: Respect for self, Respect for others. Responsibility for all your actions.
19. Don't let a little dispute injure a great friendship.
20. When you realize you've made a mistake, take immediate steps to correct it.
21. Smile when picking up the phone. The caller will hear it in your voice.
22. Marry a person you love to talk to. As you get older, his/her conversational skills will be even more important.
23. Spend some time alone.
24. Open your arms to change, but don't let go of your values.
25. Remember that silence is sometimes the best answer.
26. Read more books. Television is no substitute.
27. Live a good, honorable life. Then when you get older and think back, you'll be able to enjoy it a second time.
28. Trust in God, but lock your car.
29. A loving atmosphere in your home is the foundation for your life. Do all you can to create a tranquil, harmonious home.

Continued on next page

For Relationship

Continued from previous page

30. In disagreements with loved ones, deal only with the current situation. Don't bring up the past.
31. Don't just listen to what someone is saying. Listen to why they are saying it.
32. Share your knowledge. It's a way to achieve immortality.
33. Be gentle with the earth.
34. Pray or meditate. There's immeasurable power in it.
35. Never interrupt when you are being flattered.
36. Mind your own business.
37. Don't trust anyone who doesn't close his/her eyes when you kiss.
38. Once a year, go someplace you've never been before.
39. If you make a lot of money, put it to use helping others while you are living. It is wealth's greatest satisfaction.
40. Remember that not getting what you want is sometimes a wonderful stroke of luck.
41. Learn the rules so you know how to break them properly.
42. Remember that the best relationship is one in which your love for each other exceeds your need for each other.
43. Judge your success by what you had to give up in order to get it.
44. Live with the knowledge that your character is your destiny.

For Spiritual

I Asked The Lord To Bless You

I asked the Lord to bless you

As I prayed for you today

To guide you and protect you

As you go along your way

His love is always with you

His promises are true,

And when we give Him all our cares

You know He will see us through.

So when the road you're traveling on

Seems difficult at best

Just remember I'm here praying

And God will do the rest.

For Spiritual

Praise Him for His Grace and Mercy

A well-known speaker started off his seminar by holding up a $20 bill. In the room of 200, he asked, "Who would like this $20 bill?" Hands started going up. He said, "I am going to give this $20 to one of you." He proceeded to crumple the dollar bill up. He then asked, "Who still wants it?"

Still the hands were up in the air. "Well," he replied, "what if I do this?" And he dropped it on the ground and started to grind it into the floor with his shoe. He picked it up, now all crumpled and dirty. "Now who still wants it?" Still the hands went into the air.

"My friends, you have all learned a very valuable lesson. No matter what I did to the money, you still wanted it because it did not decrease in value. It was still worth $20. Many times in our lives, we are dropped, crumpled, and ground into the dirt by the decisions we make and the circumstances that come our way. We feel as though we are worthless. But no matter what has happened or what will happen, you will never lose your value in God's eyes. To Him, dirty or clean, crumpled or finely creased, you are still priceless."

THOUGHT: The worth of our lives comes not in what we do or what we look like, but WHO WE ARE! You are special - don't ever forget it!

Please pass this on, you will never know the lives it touches, the hurting hearts it speaks to, or the hope that it can bring!

For Spiritual

A Time To Give Up

Jenny was a bright-eyed, pretty five-year-old girl. One day when she and her mother were checking out at the grocery store, Jenny saw a plastic pearl necklace priced at $2.50. How she wanted that necklace, and when she asked her mother if she would buy it for her, her mother said, "Well, it is a pretty necklace, but it costs an awful lot of money. I'll tell you what. I'll buy the necklace, and when we get home we can make up a list of chores that you can do to pay for the necklace. And don't forget that for your birthday Grandma just might give you a whole dollar bill, too. Okay?"

Jenny agreed, and her mother bought the pearl necklace for her. Jenny worked on her chores very hard every day, and sure enough, her grandma gave her a brand new dollar bill for her birthday. Soon Jenny had paid off the pearls. How Jenny loved those pearls. She wore them everywhere: kindergarten, bed and when she went out with her mother to run errands. The only time she didn't wear them was in the shower - her mother had told her that they would turn her neck green!

Now Jenny had a very loving daddy. When Jenny went to bed, he would get up from his favorite chair every night and read Jenny her favorite story. One night when he finished the story, he said, "Jenny, do you love me?"

"Oh yes, Daddy, you know I love you," the little girl said. "Well, then, give me your pearls." "Oh! Daddy, not my pearls!" Jenny said. "But you can have Rosie, my favorite doll. Remember her? You gave her to me last year for my birthday. And you can have her tea party outfit, too. Okay?"

Continued on next page

For Spiritual

Continued from previous page

"Oh no, darling, that's okay." Her father brushed her cheek with a kiss. "Good night, little one." A week later, her father once again asked Jenny after her story, "Do you love me?" "Oh yes, Daddy, you know I love you." "Well, then, give me your pearls." "Oh, Daddy, not my pearls! But you can have Ribbons, my toy horse. Do you remember her? She's my favorite. Her hair is so soft, and you can play with it and braid it and everything. You can have ribbons if you want her, Daddy," the little girl said to her father.

"No, that's okay," her father said and brushed her cheek again with a kiss. "God bless you, little one. Sweet dreams." Several days later, when Jenny's father came in to read her a story, Jenny was sitting on her bed and her lip was trembling. "Here, Daddy," she said and held out her hand. She opened it and her beloved pearl necklace was inside. She let it slip into her father's hand.

With one hand her father held the plastic pearls and with the other he pulled out of his pocket a blue velvet box. Inside of the box were real, genuine, beautiful pearls. He had had them all along. He was waiting for Jenny to give up the cheap stuff so he could give her the real thing. So it is with our Heavenly Father. He is waiting for us to give up the cheap things in our lives so he can give us beautiful treasure. Isn't God good?

For Spiritual

The Other Side Of The Coin

I'm thankful for the taxes I pay because it means that I'm employed.

I'm thankful for the mess to clean after a party because it means I have been surrounded by friends.

I'm thankful for the clothes that fit a little too snug because it means I have enough to eat.

I'm thankful for my shadow who watches me work because it means I am out in the sunshine.

I'm thankful for a lawn that needs mowing, windows that need cleaning and gutters that need fixing becaue it means I have a home.

I'm thankful for all the complaining I hear about our government because it means we have freedom of speech.

I'm thankful for the spot I find at the far end of the parking lot because it means I am capable of walking.

I'm thankful for my huge heating bill because it means I am warm.

I'm thankful for the lady behind me in church who sings off key because it means that I can hear.

I'm thankful for the piles of laundry and ironing because it means I have clothes to wear.

I'm thankful for weariness and aching muscles at the end of the day because it means I have been productive.

I'm thankful for the alarm that goes off in the early morning hours because it means that I'm alive.

I'm thankful for getting too much email because it lets me know I have friends who are thinking of me.

For Spiritual

God's Wings

An article in National Geographic several years ago provided a penetrating picture of God's wings...

After a forest fire in Yellowstone National Park, forest rangers began their trek up a mountain to assess the inferno's damage. One ranger found a bird literally petrified in ashes, perched statuesquely on the ground at the base of a tree. Somewhat sickened by the eerie sight, he knocked over the bird with a stick. When he struck it, three tiny chicks scurried from under their dead mother's wings.

The loving mother, keenly aware of impending disaster, had carried her offspring to the base of the tree and had gathered them under her wings, instinctively knowing that the toxic smoke would rise. She could have flown to safety but had refused to abandon her babies.

When the blaze had arrived and the heat had scorched her small body, the mother had remained steadfast. Because she had been willing to die, those under the cover of her wings would live.

"He will cover you with his feathers, and under His wings you will find refuge" (Psalm 91:4).

Being loved this much should make a difference in your life. Remember the One who loves you and then be different because of it. Please pass this on to others you care about.

Naughty Boys

A couple had two little boys, ages 8 and 10, who were excessively mischievous. The two were always getting into trouble and their parents could be assured that if any mischief occurred in their town, their two young sons were in some way involved. The parents were at their wit's end as to what to do about their sons' behavior.

The mother had heard that a clergyman in town had been successful in disciplining children in the past, so she asked her husband if he thought they should send the boys to speak with the clergyman. The husband said, "We might as well. We need to do something before I really lose my temper!" The clergyman agreed to speak with the boys but asked to see them individually.

The 8-year-old went to meet with him first. The clergyman sat the boy down and asked him sternly, "Where is God?"

The boy made no response, so the clergyman repeated the question in an even sterner tone, "Where is God?"

Again the boy made no attempt to answer. So the clergyman raised his voice even more and shook his finger in the boy's face, "WHERE IS GOD?"

At that the boy bolted from the room and ran directly home, slamming himself in the closet. His older brother followed him into the closet and said, "What happened?"

The younger brother replied, "We are in BIG trouble this time. God is missing, and they think we did it."

For Spiritual

Blessings We May Not Recognize

1. If you own a Bible, you are abundantly blessed - about 1/3 of the world does not have access to one.

2. If you wake up each morning with more health than illness, you are blessed to rise and shine, to live and to serve in a new day.

3. If you have anyone on the planet, just one person who loves you and listens to you count this as a blessing.

4. If you can freely attend a church meeting without fear, then you are more blessed than over 1/3 of the world.

5. If you have a yearning in your heart to parent a child, you are blessed because you still desire what you cannot see.

6. If you pray today or any day, you are blessed because you believe in God's willingness to hear your prayer.

7. If you pray for someone else, you are blessed because you want to help others also.

8. If you have food in your refrigerator, clothes on your back, a roof over your head, and a place to sleep, all at the same time, you are rich in this world.

9. If you have a brother or sister in Christ who will pray with you and for you, you benefit from a spiritual unity, bond, and agreement, against which the gates of hell cannot stand.

10. If you have any earthly family that even halfway loves you and supports you, you are blessed beyond measure.

11. If you attend a church with a church family that offers you one word of encouragement, you are blessed with some form of fellowship.

For Spiritual

12. If you have money in the bank, in your wallet, or some spare change in a dish someplace, you are among the world's wealthy.

13. If you can go to bed each night knowing that God loves you, you are blessed beyond measure.

14. If you try each day to imitate our Lord Jesus Christ for even a minute, you are blessed because you show a willingness to grow up in Him.

15. If you can read this message, you are more blessed than about 1/3 of the world who cannot read at all.

16. If you have never had to endure the hardship and agony of battle, imprisonment, or torture, you are blessed in indescribable measure.

17. If you have a voice to sing His praises, a voice to witness God's love, and a voice to share the gospel, you are blessed. About 1/3 of the world does not even know who the one true God is.

18. If you can hold someone's hand, hug another person, touch someone on the shoulder, you are blessed because you can offer God's healing touch.

19. If you can share a word of encouragement with someone else, and do it with His love in your heart, you are blessed because you have learned how to give.

20. If you have the conviction to stand fast upon His Word and His promises, no matter what, you are blessed because you are learning patience, endurance, and tenacity.

Continued on next page

For Spiritual

Continued from previous page

21. If you hold up your head with a smile on your face and are truly thankful, you are blessed because most people can, but many will not.

How To Get In Touch

Mommy went to Heaven, but I need her here today,
My tummy hurts and I fell down, I need her right away,
Operator, can you tell me how to find her in this book?
Is heaven in the yellow part, I don't know where to look.
I think my daddy needs her too, at night I hear him cry.
I hear him call her name sometimes, but I really don't know why.
Maybe if I call her, she will hurry home to me.
Is Heaven very far away? Is it across the sea?
She's been gone a long, long time, she needs to come home now!
I really need to reach her, but I simply don't know how.
Help me find the number please, is it listed under "Heaven"?
I can't read these big big words, I am only seven.
I'm sorry operator, I didn't mean to make you cry.
Is your tummy hurting too, or is there something in your eye?
If I call my church, maybe they will know.
Mommy said when we need help that's where we should go.
I found the number to my church tacked up on the wall.
Thank you, operator I'll give them a call.

For Women

The Spelling Bee

After a long illness, a woman died and arrived at the Gates of Heaven. While she was waiting for Saint Peter to greet her, she peeked through the Gates. She saw a beautiful banquet table. Sitting all around were her parents and all the other people she had loved and who had died before her. They saw her and began calling greetings to her- "Hello"

"How are you! We've been waiting for you!" "Good to see you".

When Saint Peter came by, the woman said to him, "This is such a wonderful place! How do I get in?"

"You have to spell a word," Saint Peter told her.

"Which word?" the woman asked.

"Love."

The woman correctly spelled "Love" and Saint Peter welcomed her into Heaven.

About six months later, Saint Peter came to the woman and asked her to watch the Gates of Heaven for him that day. While the woman was guarding the Gates of Heaven, her husband arrived.

"I'm surprised to see you", the woman said. "How have you been?"

"Oh, I've been doing pretty well since you died", her husband told her. "I married the beautiful young nurse who took care of you while you were ill. And then I won the lottery. I sold the little house you and I lived in and bought a big mansion. And my wife and I traveled all around the world. We were on vacation and I went water skiing today.

Continued on next page

For Women

Continued from previous page

I fell, the ski hit my head, and here I am. How do I get in?"

"You have to spell a word," the woman told him.

"Which word?" her husband asked.

"Czechoslovakia."

The Surgery

In the hospital where their family member lay gravely ill, relatives gathered in the waiting room. Finally, the doctor came in looking tired and somber.

"I'm afraid that I'm the bearer of bad news", he said as he surveyed the worried faces. "The only hope left for your loved one at this time is a brain transplant. It's an experimental procedure, quite risky, and you'll have to pay for the brain yourselves."

The family members sat silently as they absorbed the news. At length, someone asked, "Well, how much does a brain cost?" to which the doctor quickly responded, "$2000 for a female brain, and $5000 for a male brain." The moment turned awkward.

Men in the room tried not to smile, avoiding eye contact with the women, but some actually smirked. A bloke, unable to control his curiosity, blurted out the question everyone wanted to ask, "Why is the male brain so much more?"

The doctor smiled at the childish innocence and then to the entire group said, "It's a standard pricing procedure: we have to mark the female brains down because they've been used."

For Women

The Funeral

A woman was leaving a 7-11 with her morning coffee when she noticed a most unusual funeral procession approaching the nearby cemetery. A long black hearse was followed by a second long black hearse about 50 feet behind.

Behind the second hearse was a solitary woman walking a pit bull on a leash. Behind her were 200 women walking single file. The woman couldn't stand her curiosity. She respectfully approached the woman walking the dog and said, "I am so sorry for your loss and I know now is a bad time to disturb you, but I've never seen a funeral like this. Whose funeral is it?"

The woman replied, "Well, the first hearse is for my husband." "What happened to him?"

The woman replied, "My dog attacked and killed him." She inquired further, "Well, who is in the second hearse?" The woman answered, "My mother-in-law. She was trying to help my husband when the dog turned on her."

A poignant and thoughtful moment of silence passed between the two women. "Could I borrow that dog?"

"Get at the end of the line."

What Women REALLY Want...

In a recent Harris Online poll 38,562 men across the US were asked to identify a woman's ultimate fantasy. 97.8% of the respondents said that a woman's ultimate fantasy was to have two men at once.

While this has been verified by a recent sociological study, it appears that most men do not realize that in this fantasy, one man is cooking and the other is cleaning.

For Women

You Can Tell It Is Going To Be A Rotten Day When...

You wake up face down on the pavement.

You put your bra on backwards and it fits better.

You call Suicide Prevention and they put you on hold.

You see a "60 Minutes" news team waiting in your office.

Your birthday cake collapses from the weight of the candles.

You want to put on the clothes you wore home from the party and there aren't any.

You turn on the news and they're showing emergency routes out of the city.

Your twin sister forgot your birthday.

Your car horn goes off accidentally and remains stuck as you follow a group of Hell's Angels on the freeway.

The bird singing outside your window is a buzzard.

You walk to work and find your dress stuck in to the back of your pantyhose.

You call your answering service and they tell you it's none of your business.

Your blind date turns out to be your ex-husband.

Your income tax check bounces.

You put both contact lenses in the same eye.

Your pet rock snaps at you.

Your husband says, "Good morning, Jane" and your name is Sara.

For Women

A Woman's Random Thoughts

Insanity is my only means of relaxation.

Reason to smile: Every 7 minutes of every day, someone in an Aerobics class pulls a hamstring.

Women over 50 don't have babies because they would put them down and forget where they left them.

One of life's mysteries is how a 2-pound box of chocolates can make a woman gain 5 pounds.

My mind not only wanders, it sometimes leaves completely.

The best way to forget all your troubles is to wear tight shoes.

The nice part about living in a small town is that when you don't know what you're doing, someone else does.

The older you get, the tougher it is to lose weight because by then your body and your fat are really good friends.

Just when I was getting used to yesterday, along came today.

Sometimes I think I understand everything, then I regain consciousness.

Amazing! You hang something in your closet for a while and it shrinks 2 sizes.

Skinny people irritate me. Especially when they say things like "You know sometimes I just forget to eat." Now I've forgotten my address,

Continued on next page

For Women

Continued from previous page

my mother's maiden name, my keys and several others things but I've never forgotten to eat. You have to be a special kind of stupid to forget to eat.

A friend of mine confused her valium with her birth control pills. She has 14 kids and really doesn't care.

They keep telling us to get in touch with our bodies. Mine isn't that communicative but I heard from it the other day after I said, "Body, how'd you like to go to a 6 o'clock vigorous toning class?" Clear as a bell my body said, "Listen witch, do it and die!"

I know what Victoria's Secret is! The secret is that nobody older than 30 can fit into their stuff.

If men can run the world, why can't they stop wearing neckties? How intelligent can it be to start the day by tying a noose around your neck?

Today's mighty oak is just yesterday's nut that held its ground.

Romance Tip For Women #201

When you want a man to play with you, wear a full-length black nightgown with buttons all over it. Sure it's uncomfortable. But it makes you look just like his remote control.

Female Comebacks

Man: Haven't I seen you someplace before?
Woman: Yes, that's why I don't go there anymore.

Man: Is this seat empty?
Woman: Yes, and this one will be if you sit down.

Man: Your place or mine?
Woman: Both. You go to yours, and I'll go to mine.

Man: So, what do you do for a living?
Woman: I'm a female impersonator.

Man: Hey baby, what's your sign?
Woman: Do not enter.

Man: How do you like your eggs in the morning?
Woman: Unfertilized.

Man: Your body is like a temple.
Woman: Sorry, there are no services today.

Man: I would go to the end of the world for you.
Woman: But would you stay there?

Man: If I could see you naked, I'd die happy.
Woman: If I saw you naked, I'd probably die laughing.

For Women

Through The Years...

Age 5 - I've learned that I like my teacher because she cries when we sing "Silent Night".......

Age 6 - I've learned that our dog doesn't want to eat my broccoli either.

Age 7 - I've learned that when I wave to people in the country, they stop what they are doing and wave back.

Age 9 - I've learned that just when I get my room the way I like it, Mom makes me clean it up again.

Age 12 - I've learned that if you want to cheer yourself up, you should try cheering someone else up.

Age 14 - I've learned that although it's hard to admit it, I'm secretly glad my parents are strict with me.

Age 15 - I've learned that silent company is often more healing than words of advice.

Age 24 - I've learned that brushing my child's hair is one of life's great pleasures.

Age 26 - I've learned that wherever I go, the world's worst drivers have followed me there.

Age 29 - I've learned that if someone says something unkind about me, I must live so that no one will believe it.

Age 39 - I've learned that there are people who love you dearly but just don't know how to show it.

Age 42 - I've learned that you can make someone's day by simply sending them a little note.

Age 44 - I've learned that the greater a person's sense of guilt, the greater his or her need to cast blame on others.

For Women

Age 46 - I've learned that children and grandparents are natural allies.

Age 47 - I've learned that no matter what happens, or how bad it seems today, life does go on, and it will be better tomorrow.

Age 48 - I've learned that singing "Amazing Grace" can lift my spirits for hours.

Age 49 - I've learned that motel mattresses are better on the side away from the phone.

Age 50 - I've learned that you can tell a lot about a man by the way he handles these three things: a rainy day, lost luggage, and tangled Christmas tree lights.

Age 51 - I've learned that keeping a vegetable garden is worth a medicine cabinet full of pills.

Age 52 - I've learned that regardless of your relationship with your parents, you miss them terribly after they die.

Age 53 - I've learned that making a living is not the same thing as making a life.

Age 58 - I've learned that if you want to do something positive for your children, work to improve your marriage.

Age 61 - I've learned that life sometimes gives you a second chance.

Age 62 - I've learned that you shouldn't go through life with a catchers mitt on both hands. You need to be able to throw something back.

Age 64 - I've learned that if you pursue happiness, it will elude you.

For Women

Continued from previous page

But if you focus on your family, the needs of others, your work, meeting new people, and doing the very best you can, happiness will find you.

Age 65 - I've learned that whenever I decide something with kindness, I usually make the right decision.

Age 66 - I've learned that everyone can use a prayer.

Age 72 - I've learned that it pays to believe in miracles. And to tell the truth, I've seen several.

Age 75 - I've learned that even when I have pains, I don't have to be one.

Age 82 - I've learned that every day you should reach out and touch someone. People love that human touch - holding hands, a warm hug, or just a friendly pat on the back.

Age 85 - I've learned that I still have a lot to learn.

STRESSED spelled backwards is DESSERTS.

Ways to purchase more copies of this book to share with others...

1) Ask for this book at your local books store by referencing the ISBN which is: 0-9721167-0-2.
2) Go to our web site at: www.offtheinternet.info
3) Phone in your order on our toll free order line: 866-798-9866.
4) Email us your order with your shipping, billing and credit card information to: offthenet@aol.com
5) Copy this page, fill out the information and fax it toll free to: 866-798-9869.

Name: _____
Billing Address: _____
_____
_____
Credit Card: Visa MC Discover
Card #: _____
Exp Date: _____
Signature: _____
If ship to address is different than the billing address, please fax that information as well.